THE Perfect Fit

THE Perfect Fit

Sandra K. Woods, PhD

iUniverse LLC
Bloomington

iUniverse books may be ordered through booksellers or by contacting:

iUniverse
1663 Liberty Drive
Bloomington, IN 47403
www.iuniverse.com
1-800-Authors (1-800-288-4677)

Because of the dynamic nature of the Internet, any web addresses or links contained in this book may have changed since publication and may no longer be valid. The views expressed in this work are solely those of the author and do not necessarily reflect the views of the publisher, and the publisher hereby disclaims any responsibility for them.

Any people depicted in stock imagery provided by Thinkstock are models, and such images are being used for illustrative purposes only. Certain stock imagery © Thinkstock.

ISBN: 978-1-4917-2638-9 (sc)
ISBN: 978-1-4917-2637-2 (e)

Library of Congress Control Number: 2014904977

Printed in the United States of America.

iUniverse rev. date: 5/8/2014

"To Be What We Are, And To Become What We Are Capable of Becoming, Is The Only End In Life."

—Robert Louis Stevenson

Contents

How Do the Things That We See and Hear and Touch and Smell Acquire Their Personal and Relative Meaning? 23

What is the Significance of Having a Feeling Brain that is More or Less Responsive Relative to Others? 33

Be-ing and Do-ing in Everyday Life 41

Preface

This work represents a point of view endeavor related to human temperament and its pervasive influence on everyday life. Putting pen to paper to bring it to completion has been difficult, in part, due to the passing of my friend and colleague, Willis H. Ploof, MD. We had planned to write this together. Many of the ideas and concepts contained in this work represent his legacy to me. To this I have added my own thinking and perspective, making the final product a marriage of sorts. As such the reader will find the pronouns "we" and "our" used freely in the text, for his influence is pervasive throughout this work.

Dedication

In loving memory of Willis H. Ploof, MD

Acknowledgements

I would like to thank the following for reading whole sections of the manuscript and for their many helpful comments and suggestions: Dr. William DiTullio, Clinical Psychologist, Private Practice, Bangor, Maine; Dr. Robert Hallock, Distinguished Professor, Physics Department, University of Massachusetts at Amherst; James M. Hurley and Janet Maratta.

Introduction

Almost as soon as we become aware of ourselves as separate beings, we begin to ask ourselves: Who am I? What is my place in life? Where do I fit? These are fundamental questions that each of us will struggle with at some point during our lifetime. A fortunate few will find out who they are early in life, but most will return to these questions again and again particularly during midlife when an increasing awareness of our own mortality results in a shift from a *time-since-birth* to a *time-left-to-live* perspective. Of all the natural forces that determine who and what we are, the contribution of temperament is perhaps the most profound for it is the web of meaning upon which we live our lives. In the following pages we will discover or should I say rediscover just how profound and pervasive that web is. Our journey will take us to familiar places of play and life, places that might seem strange at first, but upon seeing them again through the prism of temperament will seem, alas, like old haunts.

Being comfortable in our own skin isn't easy. Like many other aspects of life, *the grass is always greener….* Self-acceptance and appreciation are, for most of us, hard-won. On the one hand we take for granted what we have; on the other, we tend to overvalue those qualities that we don't have that we see in others. And to complicate matters, the process is confounded by the necessity of learning our parental and cultural dos and don'ts, which begins in early childhood. During this *cultural embryonic stage,* certain behaviors are "good," others are "bad," and there is little room for discussion. These are important survival lessons, but they come with a price. Out of necessity, many aspects of our individuality and freedom of expression are suppressed during this period while we acquire the gender-specific hood of childhood and learn to internalize right from wrong. As adults, we will be able to rethink these early lessons of childhood and decide for ourselves. But as youngsters we simply don't have enough experience nor are we in a position, developmentally, to use reason and logic to evaluate the fundamental *goodness* or *badness* of things. The brain structures, e.g., prefrontal cortex, underlying these skills are only beginning to mature.

If we were "better" than our siblings at internalizing parental dos and don'ts, we probably had an easier time of it. That is to say, we weren't as likely to get yelled at as often or sent to our rooms as much or lose privileges as much as they were. We were the "good," easy-to-manage, compliant child. On the other hand, we didn't have as much fun as or get noticed as much as our nonconforming, always-pushing-the-envelope sibling. Life just didn't seem fair. And we had a point, but from our nonconforming sibling's perspective, life wasn't all that fair either. All that negative attention left them feeling somehow inherently "bad".

Truth is, young humans don't have much control over whether they are difficult versus easy to manage. We are all predisposed by our genes to be more or less sensitive to the positive and negative feelings emanating from others. Other things being equal, the easier our brains are to stimulate in this regard, the easier it will be for us to tune into the subtle changes in tone of voice and facial expression that impart meaning to our actions. If all it takes is a mild glance of disapproval to inhibit the wrongful deed *before* it shows up in behavior, *we* can effectively avoid further discipline. But I'm getting ahead of myself.

Each stage of development brings its own particular challenges with respect to selfhood. As previously stated, childhood is a period of self-subjugation and conformity to outside authority as represented by parents and other significant adults. And this is not necessarily bad. To survive and take our place in society, we have to know what the rules are. Gaining control over our impulses and drives is an integral part of the process.

The onset of puberty signals the beginning of the next stage which is or should be about individuation and increasing autonomy. All too often, however, it is about rebellion and the persistence of authoritative approaches that have outlived their usefulness. It's easy to feel between a rock and a hard place during this time—neither child or adult—one foot in one world, one foot in the other. As adolescents we're still expected to toe the line in terms of our parental dos and don'ts, but sexual awakening with its many internal and external changes is stimulating a recall to the inner self. More and more, we're becoming aware of ourselves as separate beings. Among other changes, our hormones are urging us to do things that our parents might have told us were naughty. How can something that feels so good be so bad we wonder?

Increasingly, we find ourselves challenging the black and white notions of childhood, insisting on rational answers to why and who said so. Our capacity for independent thought is emerging and we want it to be recognized and accepted. We seek more freedom and privacy. No taxation without representation is our position. We rebel and our parents fight back, still wanting to protect us, still relating to us as children. Their authoritative approach is inappropriate at this stage in our development, but they, like us, are having difficulty making the transition. It's a confusing time for all. Having failed to recognize and encourage our emerging capacity for independent thought, our parents have unintentionally alienated us.

We begin to look more to our peers for direction and approval. Their opinions and attitudes take precedence in shaping our behavior. We want to fit in, to belong. It's important for our psychic and social survival. But to fit in, we have to express some behaviors and repress others. And if we arrive at this point with little or no sense of who we are as individuals, we run the risk of being unduly influenced by the expectations others have for us. It's a delicate balancing act—being oneself within the context of the group. Where to turn for direction?

What we really needed, more than anything, at this stage is the benevolent ear of a mature adult—someone who could have appreciated our need to freely question any area of life, someone who could have guided us without preaching. He or she would have had to be good at the Socratic Method—stimulating our thinking with leading questions, making us use logic and fact to back up our opinions. If we could have found this at home, there would have been little need to rebel for we would have had what we needed—the freedom to think openly for ourselves—the freedom to explore what is right and wrong for us. If we had this at home, we were among the lucky few. Many adolescents have to look elsewhere for this needed kind of mentoring.

Before too long, it will be time for us to take our place among the adults of our culture. But will we be ready? We'll have all the outward physical signs of adulthood but what about our inner development? What about our brain power? Will we possess the mature reasoning capacities of an adult mind or will we still think in the black-or-white terms of childhood? Will we finally be able to trust in our own feeling and thinking capacities, using them in concert to chart our own destiny without harming ourselves or others? Will we finally know who we are and what we want and how to achieve our goals with confidence, grace, and humanity?

This is the natural backdrop against which the search for the self evolves. The self is in part collective, and in part unique. Suffice it to say that our collective inheritance is human with all that this implies. Our individual uniqueness is conferred by the variability in our genes. Some of us have genes that make us naturally gifted in math or music or drawing, for example. A similar genetic variability underlies individual differences in temperament. Of course how and whether and to what degree we develop all the potentialities conferred by our genes is a matter of how our nature interacts with the nurture we receive during our lifetime. Someone with a natural talent for music, for example, would be more likely to express that talent in a favorable environment. But to some extent our genes bring their own pressures to bear on the environment. Denied such nurturing during childhood, this same individual may search elsewhere for opportunities to explore and develop that latent musical talent.

The interaction between nature and nurture is always two-way. This is true whether we are talking about innate talents or those heritable aspects of personality that are collectively referred to as temperament. Although to a limited extent, nurture can push our temperament around, our temperament can push right back—often with a forcefulness that overrides even the strongest attempts at suppression. Someone who is bold and oppositional by nature may *persist* in getting his or her own way in spite of the harshest attempts to dissuade. Similarly, someone who is introspective by nature may insist on withdrawing from the banquet of social experience from time to time in order to spend time alone thinking and processing their experiences. In this manner the temperaments may be said to be nurturing their natures.

Such pushes and pulls between nature and nurture are woven into the fabric of everyday life. Environment pressures act selectively and randomly—promoting at times, inhibiting at other times, the many natural potentialities within us. Again, our genes push back, propelling us—often without conscious awareness—into those specific environments that can nurture such preexisting tendencies. As we will see, one of the strongest, most pervasive forces acting upon us at any given moment is the force of our own temperament. It is a force that must be reckoned with. Although we may try to deny or hide it at times, eventually ***our temperament will out.***

As a purely theoretical construct, the notion of temperament has survived through the millenniums—a tribute to its validity and usefulness in helping us understand what it means to be us. In the next section, we'll take a brief look at this concept from an historical perspective.

Temperament: An Ancient Concept with Enduring Significance

The idea of temperament dates back to the time of Hippocrates when personality was thought to be an emergent property of the four ancient bodily humors. Depending upon the relative proportions of these fluids within the body, individuals were said to be choleric, melancholic, sanguine, or phlegmatic in nature. The choleric individual was said to possess a pugnacious, passionate and irritable nature due to an excess of yellow bile. An excess of black bile was said to be responsible for the sad, dejected and pessimistic nature of the melancholic; an excess of blood, for the confident, optimistic and energetic nature of the sanguine. And the slow, calm and deliberate demeanor of the phlegmatic type was thought to arise from a preponderance of phlegm.

Although we now know that temperament isn't rooted in blood or bile or phlegm, we still don't know for certain what makes one person naturally more quiet and shy, and another, more lively and uninhibited. And although natural differences in temperament are commonly perceived, especially by mothers and other caretakers of the young, the idea of temperament has only recently received wide acceptance by the scientific community. In the not so distant past, scientists were loath to study so-called psychical phenomena such as temperament. This was due, in part, to an enduring but antiquated notion that mental and psychical phenomena were somehow exempt from the laws governing the natural physical world. This notion severely restricted the disciplines and tools that were brought to bear on the study of personality. But thanks to modern techniques and the successful completion of the Human Genome Project, a worldwide effort to map the body's DNA, that belief is finally being replaced by one that is more in keeping with the evidence—specifically, that all mental phenomena have their material basis in the living tissue of the brain.

With respect to temperament, we now know that certain personality traits such as excitability, novelty seeking, and shyness are determined, in part, by naturally occurring variations in the *form* of a small number of genes (Ebstein, Novick, Umansky et al., 1996; Hamer & Copeland, 1998). The genes identified thus far contain the recipes for making some of the proteins that the brain uses to build two of its most important neurochemical systems. These two systems underlie human emotion. Out of one comes good feeling such as joy and comfort. Out of the other comes bad feeling such as exasperation and guilt. Scientists have aptly named the former the ***reward or pleasure*** system of the brain, and the latter, the ***punishment*** system.

The precise role of these systems in human temperament will be discussed a little later on. First, we're going to tell you about some of the functions that brain proteins fulfill and how genes get involved. This brief journey into the molecular world within will prepare you for what follows as it introduces you to one of the true miracles of nature—specifically, ***how the collective mix of behaviors and traits that makes each one of us unique,*** **arises out of the** ***collective behavior of molecules.*** For some of you, this may be a first exposure of sorts and thus a little heavy going in places. But it's impossible to talk about this world without naming a few of the major players and describing their functions using the terms that scientists have come up with. As much as possible we have tried to use plain language in all of our explanations. Our hope is that you won't skip this next chapter for it will provide you with a tangible edifice to hang your hat on as you consider the relevance of the ideas and concepts contained in this work.

2

The Nuts and Bolts of Human Temperament

Many of our core personality traits are shaped long before we emerge from the womb. This innate aspect of personality—our temperament—is one of our most enduring features. Although it may be modified, to some extent over the course of our lifetime, it is seldom extinguished. Like other inborn traits, our temperament is determined by instructions carried within our genes. In this case, genes direct the building of specific brain proteins that give our temperament its unique form. How our genes accomplish this feat is the subject of this chapter.

The Protein-Behavior Connection

The notion that proteins and behavior are related can seem, at first, like the stuff of science fiction. But proteins are, in large measure, what make us tick for they underlie most of the life-sustaining processes that go on inside us. The proteins of the body, like the proteins that we eat, are large molecules constructed from smaller molecules called *amino acids*. Although they are cut from the same fabric so-to-speak as ordinary dietary protein, the protein molecules of living organisms are anything but ordinary. Unlike their passive, inanimate cousins, these molecular giants have a life. Moving to the beat of their own drum, they react and behave in specialized fashion according to instructions choreographed by our genes passed down through our ancestors. They can stretch like rubber, spin like wheels, and stick like glue. They can grab onto things and carry things and store things. They can build things up and tear things down and even edit. They can hunt down invading microbes and destroy them before they have a chance to destroy us. Some underlie our thinking, others, our memory. Some work as hormones and some, as enzymes. Still others cooperate with fellow proteins to create complex factories that produce substances that allow one brain cell to communicate with another. Diverse in form and function, these dynamic, molecular entities are, in large measure, the material us—ranking second only to water in terms of all the ingredients that make up a living, feeling, behaving human.

At this very moment, your very own protein making machinery is busy at work building and rebuilding many of these molecules. Each one will be pieced together one amino acid at a time in a precise sequence from instructions encoded in your genome. In finished form, they will fold into intricate, complex shapes. Some will look like horseshoes, some like propellers, still others, like barrels. Many will aggregate with other proteins to form gigantic, cooperative, working complexes. Together with their helper molecules—things like vitamins and minerals and ATP, the energy-powering molecule of the body—these large conglomerates will transform into the visible flesh and sinew of the body and brain.

Laboratories in many countries are working hard on a collective effort to identify the structure and function of the entire complement of proteins encoded in the human genome. This world-wide effort will no doubt turn out be as big as, if not bigger than, all of the energies that were brought to bear on the Human Genome Project. This endeavor even has a name—The Human Proteome Project—and its official announcement came shortly after the announcement, in the year 2000, that the human genome had finally been identified. But more importantly, at least in terms of the present discussion, is that our temperament—the heritable component of our personality—emerges out of the collective behavior of a small number of these molecular-sized dynamos each having a different yet complementary function to fulfill. Scientists still haven't identified all of the proteins involved, but we do know the functions of those identified thus far. They work as enzymes, as receptors, and as transporters. *And, as we will see, the way that they behave influences the way that we behave.*

Behaving Brain Proteins: Enzymes, Receptors, and Transporters

Enzymes

Of all the many important functions fulfilled by the proteins of the brain, the role of enzyme is perhaps the most vital. *Enzymes are biochemical catalysts* whose function is to speed up the myriad of neurochemical reactions taking place within the cells of the brain at any given moment. Without enzymes, the biochemical reactions of the body and brain would take place far too slowly to sustain life.

Along with their catalytic function, enzymes *help to transform one substance into another.* They break down complex substances into simpler ones. They also piece together parts of small molecules to make larger molecules. To accomplish this job, enzymes *gather* all of the necessary ingredients together in close proximity, positioning them just so, making it easier for them to interact.

When I try to picture how enzymes stitch together small molecules to make bigger ones, I imagine the long segmented body of a caterpillar fully extended and laying on its side with its tiny feet exposed to and sensing the surroundings, selectively grabbing onto various substances in its immediate environment. Then I imagine the fluid motion of the caterpillar, bending and contorting its body this way and that—using this gross movement and the finer movements of its little feet to position the individual substances close enough together so that they can actually touch. Enzymes behave in analogous fashion. First they unfold, exposing certain portions of themselves to the surrounding environment. Then these exposed active sites grab onto the various small molecules that the enzyme will use in the reaction. This binding of small molecules actually changes the conformation of the enzyme. Specifically, the enzyme bends and folds in such a way that positions the bound ingredients together in close proximity. In chemistry, reactions occur when two or more molecules collide. Enzymes make sure the necessary collisions occur—kind of like a friend setting us up with a blind date and waiting for the sparks to fly.

Among the molecules that enzymes help to piece together are classes of small molecules called **neurotransmitters**. The cells of the brain use neurotransmitters to *talk* to one another. They do so by ferrying messages across the synapse—a tiny gap that exists between one brain cell and another. It's kind of like boarding a ferry to deliver mail from Long Island to the Connecticut shoreline. To give you some idea of how important enzymes and neurotransmitters are in the scheme of things, consider the following: without a specialized enzyme known as tyrosine hydroxylase, the neurons of the reward system wouldn't be able to produce the neurotransmitter, **dopamine**, the brain's pleasure molecule. Whenever we feel good inside, it's because quantities of this small molecule have been released into the reward system of the brain.

Receptors

Another important function subserved by brain proteins is that of receptor. Receptors are located on the outer membranes of brain cells. Their job is to *recognize* a specific neurochemical in the fluids that bathe the cells of the brain, capture and hold onto it for a specified time. The coupling of neurochemical and receptor changes how brain cells behave in important and diverse ways. In some cases it dampens or inhibits the cells activity. In other cases, it excites the cell, stirring it up, causing it to fire off a specific message to the other cells and structures that lie along its pathway.

The brain has many different types of neurochemical receptors. Many of the medications used to treat depression and other forms of psychic illness target the receptor proteins of brain cells. The medications are able to alter the functioning of the brain cells they bind to because they are tailor-made to fit. Put another way, the receptor is able to recognize and hold onto the drug molecule because the structure of the drug, or at least some critical part of its structure, is similar to the structure of the neurochemical that it normally binds.

An example of a widely used substance that interacts with brain receptors in this fashion is nicotine. Because nicotine's structure is similar to a naturally occurring neurochemical called acetylcholine, it is able to be bound by one of the acetylcholine receptors. Named after the drug it binds, these nicotinic receptors are found in considerable quantity on the outer membranes of dopamine neurons. When nicotine docks onto these receptor sites, dopamine cells are excited and release little packets of dopamine molecules into the reward pathways of the brain. Although we can't actually feel these packets being released, subjectively we "know" what the cell is doing because it registers as an inner feeling of pleasure. Nicotine has other effects in the brain, but the one that makes us feel good inside is mediated by dopamine.

Transporters

The last function that we will discuss is that of transporter. Transporter proteins are found embedded in the membranes of cells. Unlike receptors, which sit on the outer surfaces of brain cells, transporters are positioned so that they penetrate through the entire membrane that surrounds the cell. Like their name implies, transporters carry specific chemical substances into and out of brain cells. Transporters (also known as membrane pumps) are necessary because there are some substances that can't pass through the lipid bilayer of the outer cell membrane without assistance. In this case, transporters provide a helping hand.

An example of a small, but very important molecule that can't get into brain cells without help, is the amino acid *tyrosine*. Some of you may already be familiar with tyrosine for it is commonly sold as a dietary supplement in many health food stores. Tyrosine belongs to a group of amino acids called *essential amino acids*, so named because the major source of these nutrients comes from the protein that we eat. Tyrosine has a special significance with respect to our emotions for it serves as the precursor molecule to dopamine, which, as previously mentioned, is the brain's pleasure molecule. After we do our part and replenish the body's stores of this important nutrient by eating, it becomes the task of a transporter to carry it across the blood-brain barrier and get it into the fluids that bathe the cells of the brain. At this point another transporter takes over and carries tyrosine inside the cell where it is chemically transformed by the enzyme, tyrosine hydroxylase, into the neurotransmitter, dopamine.

Now here comes the next critical point—*the biochemical behavior of a protein is directly related to its three-dimensional structure*. Change the structure, even slightly, and you may seriously compromise the ability of a protein to carry out its job. The next section provides the explanation.

What is the Relationship between Form and Function?

In order to understand the answer to this question, it is necessary to know something about how proteins are made. As previously noted, proteins are large molecules constructed from smaller molecules called amino acids. Amino acids can be thought of as the basic building blocks of all proteins. There are twenty different amino acids stored in the tissues of the body which come from the process of digestion—the chopping up of dietary protein by digestive enzymes into small, absorbable pieces. When the time comes to construct a particular protein—perhaps to replace that has been destroyed by wear and tear, a muscle protein for example, the protein making machinery of the cell will select what it needs from the bodies stores. Most amino acids are readily available for they are present in abundance in the body's coffers, but some are present in such small quantities that supplies must be replenished frequently from the diet. These are the previously described essential amino acids.

After all of the basic building blocks are carried inside the cell by their respective transports, who or what does the building? The answer is that each cell of the brain houses the necessary equipment for building all of the various enzymes, receptors, transporters and other protein molecules that it will need during its life span. This protein manufacturing machine is itself a gigantic protein complex called a *ribosome* consisting of two large sub-units each containing several protein chains together with transfer RNA (ribonucleic acid), messenger RNA, and ATP (adenosine tri-phosphate). Ribosomes make all of the various proteins needed by the cell. Although different brain cells have their specific protein requirements, the way this machinery works is essentially the same for each cell. Specifically, instead of mixing the constituent amino acids together like the ingredients of a cake, each constituent amino acid is carefully selected and then added to the growing molecule one at a time in a precise order much like individual pearls may be added onto the chain of a necklace.

In finished form, some of these chains are quite large, containing hundreds and even thousands of amino acids. Obviously, our cells can't build such enormous molecules from only twenty possible choices so some of the ingredients must be used over again. And this is precisely what happens. As a general rule, each of the twenty amino acids is represented at least once in the chain or multiple times depending upon the particular protein recipe.

Proteins Come in Globs

Although all proteins are constructed in this same linear fashion, they do not come in linear shapes. A finished protein is irregular or globular in form. This is because the bonds that hold the amino acids together on the chain, although strong, still allow the individual amino acids to rotate around the bond—much like the pearls of a necklace are free to swivel around the chain of the necklace. This freedom of movement brings near and far amino acids on the chain into close proximity. As it happens, weak but significant attractive bonds form when particular amino acids on the chain come close together. These weak attractive forces cause the chain to bend and fold, back and forth, naturally and without assistance into an intricate three-dimensional shape. Each protein molecule has a particular "stable" conformation. This conformation is a direct result of the sequence of amino acids within the chain. In a way a finished protein molecule is like a finished pearl necklace all in a clump. Some of these "clumps" contain more than one strand—all intertwined like the many intricate twists of a gigantic torsade.

Now here is another important point: *in order to behave properly, proteins must be properly shaped*. Two proteins can contain the same number and kinds of amino acids, but if even one of these amino acids is put into the growing chain at a different place, this "minor" difference may be sufficient to completely alter its structure and therefore its biochemical behavior. To give you some idea of just how important sequence is to shape and shape is to biochemical behavior, consider the disease known as sickle cell anemia. This disease arises out of a mutation (a "mistake") in one of the genes that code for the hemoglobin molecule. Specifically, one of the protein chains in the molecule (the beta-chain) contains the amino acid, valine, at a position that is normally occupied by an amino acid known as glutamic acid. This *point substitution* modifies the spatial configuration of the molecule, sharply reducing its ability to bind and carry oxygen. Even the red blood cells of the body are themselves transformed by this change in hemoglobin. Instead of assuming their normal rounded configuration, they take on a sickle shape. These distorted sickle cells don't function properly. They get stuck in capillaries and impede the flow of blood throughout the body.

To further drive home the importance of form to function, let's look again at one of the most important classes of proteins built by the cells of the brain: enzymes. Recall that one of the functions of an enzyme is to gather together all of the various ingredients that will be needed to convert a bunch of smaller molecules into one larger molecule. To accomplish this tasks, certain amino acids must be positioned just so within the enzyme molecule. It is this spatial positioning that allows the enzyme to grab onto the individual ingredients and align them just so in order that they may interact properly. If this positioning is faulty or disrupted in any way, the enzyme will not work and one of the life-sustaining processes within the cell will grind to a halt.

Finally, given that sequence determines shape and shape determines functioning, one final question arises: ***How does the protein-making machinery of the cell know what sequence to use?*** Put another way, who or what "tells" the cell what specific amino acids to use, how often to use them, in what order and under what conditions? This is where our genes come in.

Genes are Key

Genes determine the sequence of amino acids within proteins. In order to understand how they do this, it is necessary to introduce you to another major player in this molecular world. The name of this player is *deoxyribonucleic acid* or **DNA.** DNA has been called life's most important molecule and this is the stuff genes are made of.

DNA is found in the nucleus of all cells in the form of two extremely long intertwining complementary strands of small molecules called **nucleotides** that are coiled around specialized protein bodies called **histones**. There are four different nucleotides: **quinine, thymine, cytosine and adenine**. Each occurs multiple times within each strand. The histones in DNA serve a specialized function unrelated to heredity. Specifically, histones are to DNA like spools are to thread. They keep the molecule tightly wrapped. In its uncoiled form, DNA would never fit inside the cell's tiny nucleus. It is simply too large.

As humans our cells contain exactly twenty three of these double-stranded, coiled molecules or twenty three pairs of chromosomes. Located within these strands are all the necessary instructions, inherited from our parents and coded in the language of nucleotides, for building and rebuilding all of the many proteins needed to sustain us during our lifetime. Each cell of the body has the same set of genes with one major exception—that of our immune system. Our immune system contains their own unique set of genes, genes which are continually evolving (mutating) during the course of our lifetime to handle the enormous number and variety of pathogens (viruses and bacteria) that we encounter. Each one of us has a unique immune system with its own unique set of evolving genes.

A Collection of Protein Recipes

A common way of thinking about DNA is that it is an enormous cookbook full of recipes for making thousands of different proteins. We could also say that DNA functions as a template, a code book, or a collection of blueprints; all of these analogies apply. Now that we have this general conceptual hook to hang our thinking caps on, we are ready to define what a gene is. *A gene is that portion (or portions) within the DNA strand that contains the recipe for making one part of a complete protein*. This definition is much broader than the classical description of a gene in which one gene was thought to code for one complete protein. A gene is still considered to be a continuous segment of DNA but the totality of segments coding for one specific protein can be widely spaced within the DNA strand. Also, this makes it possible for one segment to be used as part of the recipe for another protein. Put simply, genes come in pieces and these pieces can be put together in different combinations to make different, but related, proteins.

But that is only part of the story. A gene is more than this. A gene also includes that part of the DNA molecule that determines when and where and under what circumstances a particular protein will be made, and even how much of it will be made. In molecular biology this aspect of gene functioning is known as *gene expression*. During our lifetime genes are routinely switching on and off in response to, among other things, environmental demands—to all of the many external influences that affect us during our lifetime: our parents, our teachers, significant others, the books we read, the music we listen to, the pathogens we encounter.

The Neurochemical Systems Underlying Temperament

Earlier we introduced you to the brain's pleasure molecule, dopamine. We said that dopamine is a major player in the reward system of the brain, one of two crucial systems forming the underlying basis of human temperament. As previously noted, dopamine ferries the message of pleasure from one cell in the pathway to the next. Whenever we feel good inside, rest assured, dopamine is at work.

Another crucial system in this dyad is the punishment system of the brain. Although the major neurotransmitter(s) involved in transmitting this inner bad feeling has yet to be definitively identified, we do know that psychically painful messages are opposing and complementary to the pleasurable messages carried by dopamine. Moreover, they are just as vital to our everyday functioning.

Working in concert, the pleasure and punishment systems of the brain make it possible for us to internalize the lessons of experience—to learn "right" from "wrong," "good" from "bad". As a unit we can think of them as subserving our internal moral compass. Together they impart meaning to the people, ideas, and events in our lives.

To recap: the brain has more than one neurotransmitter substance and more than one neurotransmitter system. And thousands of different proteins go into the making of these systems. We said that two of these systems comprise the underlying basis of human temperament. They are the reward and punishment systems of the human brain and the messages carried by these systems are respectively, ones of psychic pleasure and ones of psychic pain. We introduced you to some of the most important proteins that determine how these systems behave—to enzymes and receptors and transporters. We learned that our genes direct the building of these proteins by translating the sequence of nucleotides within a portion (or portions) of the DNA molecule into specific sequences of amino acids. And we learned that sequence determines shape and that shape determines function. *In the final analysis, it is these functional differences that matter.*

From Genetic Architecture to Temperament Type

Due to slight variations in the set or combination of genes that code for the reward and punishment systems of the brain, humans inherit reward and punishments systems that behave differently. These differences are reflected in the combination of observable traits and behaviors that distinguish one temperament type from another. One of the genes found to be associated with individuals who are high in a trait known as novelty seeking, for example, is the dopamine D4 receptor gene (Benjamin, J., Li L., Patterson, C., et al., 1996). Because of slight variations in this gene, the D4 receptor comes in slightly different shapes.

If our D4 receptors were all alike, i.e., had the same form, each one of us might be predisposed, so to speak, to behave in similar fashion with respect to novelty seeking. But we don't. Some of us have genes that say, in effect, make this particular receptor protein, but be sure to use the elongated version of the recipe, i.e., use more amino acids and more repeats of the same amino acid sequence within a portion of the chain. As it turns out, individuals who inherit the longer version of the dopamine D4 receptor gene have receptors that are "less sensitive" to dopamine. In other words, because of its elongated shape, the receptor doesn't grab onto the dopamine molecule as well. These are the individuals who tend to be high in the trait of novelty seeking (also called thrill seeking), whereas those with the shorter version of the gene tend to be low.

This natural genetic variability is at the core of human temperament. This doesn't mean that nurture doesn't have an important role to play, rather that genes play a critical role too, one that has been largely minimized until recently. In the final analysis, nature and nurture come together to shape our personality. Nature provides the predisposition and nurture affects whether or not the trait is expressed and with what intensity. Someone who had inherited all the genes for novelty seeking, for example, would be more prone to express it depending, of course, upon upbringing and all of the other social and cultural influences acting at the time. But the interaction is two-way. Our nature can push our nurture around too as we will see in the upcoming chapters.

Scientists still have a lot of work to do before they will be able to tell us precisely what genes and proteins shape our temperament. As previously noted, in April of 2000, a sequel to The Human Genome Project was announced called The Human Proteome Project which has as its goal, the identification of all of the several thousands of proteins encoded in the human genome. Within the next several years we should know a good deal more about the genetic and proteomic basis of temperament. The notion of human temperament has certainly come a long way from its *humorous* origins.

Putting it all Together

In a previous work (Woods & Ploof, 1997), we defined temperament as the ***emotional template upon which all of our activity is superimposed***, and I am still partial to this interpretation. This template is part of our genetic makeup, a gift from our mammalian ancestors, and as we shall see, its function is to impart personal and relative meaning to our experiences. Its organic basis can be found deep within the human brain within the reward and punishment circuits or what we collectively refer to as ***the feeling brain***. Stimulation of the feeling brain transforms the cold light with which we see into the warm light with which we feel. Such transformations subserve our subjective feelings of psychic pain and psychic pleasure—simple good and bad feeling—from the pleasurable sensations associated with a comfortable pair of slippers, to the unpleasant feelings of guilt and shame.

As we go about our daily lives, our feeling brain is continually active, imprinting the events, ideas, objects, and people in our lives with good or bad feeling. This process is automatic—as natural as seeing and hearing. Without it, we would be lost. Our physical and psychic survival depends upon it. But as it happens, some of us are better imprinters than others by nature. And this difference is at the heart of our conceptualization of human temperament for there are important aspects to our behaving and thinking and relating that depend upon how deeply or lightly we imprint. But before we discuss the why and the how of this, let's explore psychic feeling in greater detail.

3

Four Basic Qualities Common to all Feeling

When we think of psychic feeling, we usually think of the full gamut of emotions: love, hate, joy, guilt, elation, remorse, and so forth. But there are certain basic qualities that are common to all feeling. These qualities are defined and illustrated below using examples from everyday life.

Fitting

The feeling of fitting is universal and refers to the yes or no of psychic feeling. Whether we are aware of it or not, we are continually asking ourselves: Does it fit? This question is related to all aspects of daily living—from the clothes we wear, to the words we use, to the people that we associate with, to the everyday solutions that we come up with to deal with the problems in our lives. Who can tell us, for example, when the shoe fits—our spouse, the store clerk, our friend? Arriving in our mind as a single answer, but based upon a multitude of sensations, only we can answer this question with a yes or a no. In this sense, fitting answers are idiosyncratic and synonymous with an inner feeling of comfort. Fitting answers make us feel good inside.

Fitting is fundamental in nature and in culture. In the natural world, molecules will bind to each other to form more complex molecules only if they fit. To be fit is to be healthy. Unfit connotes illness, lack of ability, lack of a suitable place. In society, fitting is linked to sanity. When our behavior suits an occasion, all will agree, we are sane. When we act in inappropriate ways, our sanity is questioned. To be fit is to be in harmony with ourselves and others.

Bonding

Bonding is akin to fitting but is greater in magnitude. ***Bonding is the super glue of psychic feeling*** and it is both instinctual and psychic. Instinctual bonding is easily observed between mothers and newborns as well as between sexual partners.

Bonding ties people, events, objects, and ideas securely together over time. Without bonding, our thinking, the events in our lives, our relationships with others would appear fragmented like a series of discrete happenings unrelated in time and substance. Such fragmentation is a symptom of psychic illness. In psychiatry, there is a phenomenon known as loose associations. Someone with loose associations jumps from one topic or thought to the next without any connecting links between ideas. Although we all do this occasionally, this becomes cause for concern when it is extreme—when it characterizes our behavior. An individual with this problem may be said to lack the glue of psychic feeling linking one thought to another.

At the opposite pole, we have ***complexes***. A complex is ***a group of thoughts and external events tied together by strong feeling***. If the feeling is negative in quality, thoughts which are apt to remind us of the event may be repressed—held at bay outside the threshold of conscious awareness. On the other hand, if the feeling is positive in quality, we may enjoy discussing it with friends or reliving it in memory. If a person enjoyed photography, for example, we might say that she or he had a photography complex. Objects and happenings and thoughts related to taking pictures would all be bound together by the feelings of inner pleasure associated with this interest. As the photographer strolled along the avenue, his or her eye would tend to pick up anything related to this interest—sales on supplies or equipment, ideal scenic compositions, and so forth. All of these stimuli—of paramount interest to the photographer—would not necessarily be noticed by the other pedestrians. In this sense, we might say that the photographer's view of the world is selective or that it has become colored by this strongly pleasurable interest. Anything related is quickly perceived while the irrelevant is easily ignored. But take this to the extreme and we again encounter psychic illness—complexes so profoundly imprinted with psychic felling that every current happening is seemingly related. In this case we might say that the individual's view of the world is paranoid or irrational.

When we think of ties that bind, we typically think of positive feeling states. But binding forces are at work in negative feeling states as well for we are as strongly bound to those we hate as to those we love. Consider the enduring antipathy and feuding that can exist between neighbors of different ethnic or religious backgrounds. For each participant in the bond, there is an enemy who must be destroyed in spirit if not in flesh. Great religious wars have been fought over such strongly held beliefs and attitudes—beliefs tightly bound and fixed in memory by the glue of psychic feeling. The events associated with September 11th, 2001 have now unwillingly bound us as a nation to those responsible.

The energy tied up in such bonds may be of great magnitude, akin to the attractive and repellant forces that bind atoms together in a molecule. This is most apparent when one of the bonded parties ceases to exist as typified by the death of a loved one. In this case, the surviving party has lost a part of the self, but also the place where their feelings have been poured and stored. Until such feelings are reattached or redirected into other endeavors, they are returned to and accumulated by the self who may be so pressed down by their weight that movement becomes impossible. This is the essence of depression for which treatment may be necessary.

The return of psychic energy to the self can be very uncomfortable indeed. Finding an external focal point can help relieve the discomfort and intensity of the feeling as typified by the individual on the rebound from an unhappy love affair. Although the self may be relieved of its burden in this case, the rebound attachment of psychic energy is made in haste without due consideration. Sooner or later, the question of fitting will arise; depending upon the answer, the new relationship may not endure.

On the other hand we may see great excitement and joy following the release of energy previously invested in a negative bond. Consider the outpouring of positive emotion, the dancing in the streets, the joyous exuberance captured on the faces of thousands of Americans on V-E day following the announcement of the end of World War II.

Bonding is also apparent in the world of ideas and problem solving. As previously noted, whenever we try to answer the what, and the how, and the why of something, the answers we come up with have to fit. Questions always push the mind for fitting solutions. They are the light switches of the brain. Often someone will strongly defend a wrong answer because of the discomfort that would follow an admission that the answer doesn't fit. To be right, the answer must fit. Ideally, the world of ideas and problem solving is one of creativity and freedom. Too often, however, it is a world of prejudice.

Prejudice is the normal state of the child's mind as the brain of a child has yet to reach its full capacity for individual thought. As children, we are in the position of having to accept the goods and the bads from parental dictums and attitudes and live accordingly. As we approach adolescence, however, the brain structures subserving independent thought are getting ready to make their contribution. Although not fully developed, adolescents strongly demand that this fledgling capacity be recognized, often to the consternation of parents who may have failed to recognize the emergence of the important developmental milestone.

When prejudice is encountered in an adult, it may indicate stagnation in the capacity for true independent thought, either because the goods and the bads learned as a child have never been reconsidered for their meaning and fitness in the present. The failure of large populations of adults to question prevailing dogma for its meaning and fitness underlies, in part, the rise of many political and religious fanatics. Eric Fromm's ***Escape From Freedom*** (1965, 1st Avon Printing), written during the rise of Hitler in Nazi Germany, comes immediately to mind. Freedom is a double-edge sword. To be free in the purest sense, one would have to be comfortable with one's essential aloneness. This more mature kind of inner freedom can be intensely anxiety provoking, akin to free-floating in the universe without a tether—physical or psychic. To escape such anxiety, many give up the struggle, blindly submitting to the ideology and dogmatic thinking of others in positions of power and authority. This may relieve their inner sense of aloneness and isolation, but it also prevents them from maturing into adults who can independently evaluate the essential goodness or badness of a particular ideology or action. According to Fromm, such a dynamic was played out in the Germany of WWII where great masses willingly gave themselves over to totalitarian rule.

Ideally speaking, the adult mind is free to question any area of knowledge. Given any topic of interest, the questions of why, what, and how must be answered. Facts must be gathered and observations made with respect to the fitting of relationships between idea and facts. With time and confidence, answers will arrive as insights—views from within. Such moments often arrive unexpectedly, intruding upon the activity of the moment or awakening us from sleep. "Eureka!" expresses our feeling at the moment of discovery.

Weight

Feelings carry weight—*that quality that depresses and elevates mood*. They can be light and buoy us up or heavy and weigh us down. At one extreme, the weight of psychic feeling can be heavy indeed, akin to being pressed deeper and deeper into a black hole where darkness surrounds and escape appears impossible. Activity slows to a snail's pace. Even the smallest of chores overwhelms. The pencil takes on the weight of a lead pipe. Our thinking becomes heavy and ponderous; our efforts to concentrate, Herculean. At the other extreme, we may be elated by positive feeling—unable to settle down as when some event suddenly releases us from our worries and fears. Metaphorically, we have hit the jackpot. Our mood becomes light and gay with arms waving, feet dancing, eyes and face alive with radiant energy. Each day may bring short-lived gradations between these two extremes of weight—the ups and downs of everyday life.

Contagion

Contagion refers to *the rapid, non-verbal communication of psychic feeling between individuals in close proximity,* as typified in the extreme by the energy transmission evident in the collective behavior of a crowd. Here we see individuals caught up in and swept away by the mood of the moment resulting in conduct that may or may not be fitting. Consider, for example, the stock market crash of the 1920s when an attitude of fear and panic prevailed, setting the stage for "the great depression" of the 1930s.

Contagion is also at work when we suddenly find, for example, that our pleasant mood had disappeared in the presence of our irritable companion, or conversely, that the humor and laughter of a friend has suddenly transformed our sadness. Put simply, feelings emanating from others can stimulate similar feeling states within us.

Closing Comments

We all need to experience the warmth of human feeling no matter what the tenor. Such feeling is as essential to our emotional health and well-being as food is to our physical health and well-being. Without it, we feel cold and empty inside. Without it, there is a regression toward infancy and perhaps even death.

4

How Do the Things That We See and Hear and Touch and Smell Acquire Their Personal and Relative Meaning?

Opening Comments

The human brain is extremely intricate in design. With over 10 billion cells, it's a kind of microscopic universe. That we understand as much about it as we do is amazing considering that it was only in the twentieth century that researchers had the tools to begin exploring this fascinating world. Trying to make sense out of the complex of cells and neurochemicals that inhabit this universe isn't easy. As new discoveries emerge, they must be named and explained and the plethora of scientific terminology that follows can overwhelm even the most seasoned of scientists. Modern neuroscience and modern genetics are virtual thickets of jargon. But when it comes right down to it, these thickets are simply a bunch of fancy words and abstractions that, for the most part, can be translated into plain language. So, as much as possible, plain language is what you will find as we attempt to simplify how the things that we see and hear and touch and smell acquire their personal and relative meaning.

Sensation

The job of extracting information from the outside world begins with external sensory receptors—the rods and cones of the retina, the tiny hair cells of the inner ear, the olfactory receptors of the nose, and so forth. Sensory receptors are modality-specific in the information they convey to the brain. This is just a fancy way of saying that receptors have their preferences in terms of what turns them on. The rods and cones of the retina respond to light wares, the sensory receptors of the ear to sound waves, and so forth. Receptors transform the signals they receive into electrochemical messages that are passed on to the higher centers of the brain where they are integrated into meaningful perceptions. Each sensory system—vision, hearing, touch, smell, taste, et cetera—has a corresponding set of receptors, neurons, pathways and brain structures that work together to process the signals arriving from the outside world. At any given point in time there are literally millions of neurons sending coded messages through the highways and byways of the brain. Even when we sleep our receptors are at work, monitoring the surrounding environment.

In order for a sensory signal to register in our conscious awareness, there is a certain threshold of stimulation that must be reached. This is, it takes a certain intensity of stimulation to turn a receptor on in the first place. This threshold of sensitivity can vary from person to person for a variety of reasons, due to nature (genetic wiring) as well as nurture, e.g., the amount of sleep you've had during the previous night. It is important to keep this in mind because we often tend to act as if we all had the same sensitivity to external stimuli. On a purely intellectual level we know better.

For arguments sake, let's assume all of our sensory receptors are working within some "normal" range of sensitivity. What happens next? How does the human brain transform an external sensory stimulus into some "usable" form or percept? Webster defines percept as the conscious impression of an object obtained through the use of the senses. The process of forming a percept is called perception. Perception is several steps removed from sensory stimulation. It requires the participation of the so-called higher brain regions—those lying upstream from the external sensory receptors.

Perception

Because humans are largely visual animals, compared to dogs or cats, for example, where smell predominates, we will use the human visual system to illustrate what goes into perception.

The brain uses the electrochemical signals arriving from the retina for a number of different functions, some having little or nothing to do with seeing. Such uses depend upon the special capacities of the cells that inhabit the places (brain structures) that these signals visit as they travel along visual pathways of the brain. An important port-of-call is the **hypothalamus**. Some of the resident cells of the hypothalamus use the signals arriving from the retina to regulate the body's circadian rhythms—natural variations in the levels of hormones and other chemicals that occur during a normal day/night cycle. Further upstream lies a structure called the **pretectum**. The pretectum is the seat of the pupillary light reflex. When the light entering the eye is too intense, the cellular inhabitants of the pretectum send feedback signals to the muscles of the eye which causes the pupil to constrict.

But the most important pathway, in terms of our discussion, is the one that begins in the retina, stops at a structure known as the **lateral geniculate nucleus of the thalamus** (the major relay station for all sensory signals arriving from the internal and external world), then continues on to the primary visual cortex located at the very back of the head. This is the pathway that underlies what we commonly call visual perception.

The visual cortex is the "big cheese" of perception. Whereas some places are mere whistle stops in terms of size (not importance), the visual cortex is an entire metropolis—the "New York City" of perception. This is the place where all the separate bits of sensory information are integrated into complete pictures or percepts. Function networks of cells residing within the various layers of the visual cortex work together as a team to make these perceptions possible. Some members of the team process color information, some contribute information about the contrast between light and dark regions of the objects in our field of vision, still others tell us about the object's angle or orientation, and whether or not it is moving or stationary.

But there is much more to perception than this. To be able to discriminate the correct spatial relationship between the various parts of the whole, information from the visual cortex must be relayed to networks of cells lying in an adjacent region of the brain called the parietal lobe. Further, should you wish to actually name the object that you perceived, the cooperation of networks of cells residing the adjacent temporal lobe would also have to be recruited.

To give you some intuitive feeling for these separate but interrelated aspects of visual perception, consider the common frustration of not being able to recall the name of a familiar person you can "see" in your mind's eye. In neuroscience jargon, this difficulty is called anomia. The disturbance lies somewhere along the path connecting specific cell networks in the visual cortex with their partner networks in the temporal cortex. Luckily, for most of us, the anomia is temporary. Sooner or later the missing name comes to mind, often with any further conscious effort on our part. We are immediately relieved. Our mind it put at ease and we are free to go to work on other matters.

Okay. So now we have percepts. Where do they live and how do we access them?

Memory Banks

Percepts are stored in memory. Some are kept there for a short time and quickly forgotten. Some make a strong enough impression to be retained for the long-term. We like to think of memory as a kind of bank or repository full of meaningful currency—a collection, if you will, of sensory impressions complexed with good or bad feeling, a place where we can go to whenever the situation dictates, whenever we want to compare past and present and thus determine our behavior in the future. Although the creation, retention and recall of a specific sensory experience involves cooperation between many subdivisions of the brain, for purposes of our discussion, it is useful to think of our sensory memories as having a home in the corresponding sensory-association cortex. The word "association" just means that sensory pathways ultimately lead to specific destinations in the cortex or the outer most layers of the brain—those lying closest to the skull. Thus we can speak of having a visual memory bank which is located in the visual cortex, an auditory memory bank which is located in the temporal cortex and so forth.

Thus far we've confined our discussion to getting sensory information from the external world into the brain in some "useable" form. Obviously complex human behavior involves much more than perception. There is thought and planning, motor execution and evaluation, and, of course, emotional coloration. Also, we've said nothing about the influences that can be exerted by the higher brain regions on sensation and ultimately, perception. We'll have more to say about this later but for now to give you some idea of what it means to alter sensation and perception from the inside, consider the individual who is surrounded by noise yet is still able to be totally engrossed in whatever he or she is doing at the moment—whether it be reading a book or playing a game of cards. The process by which our brain is able to tune out or dampen our responsiveness to signals arriving from the outside world is called **habituation.** Another way of saying this is we "get used to" irrelevant stimuli—they fade into the background. However, should a sudden loud noise interrupt our concentration we would be immediately altered turning our attention toward the source, checking it out for familiarity and meaning. Our brain does this automatically. Scientists call this process the ***orienting reflex***.

To recap: perception is a complex process involving much more than the reception of a sensory signal from the outside world. Many players have a hand in transforming a simple sensory stimulus into a complex perception—one that can be processed into memory, one that we can return to again and again whenever we want to, whenever the situation dictates. Ultimately all of the players involved in the transformation must work together as a team to get the job done. This ability to work in concert is subserved by the many functional connections between the component parts.

The link that we are most concerned about for this writing, however, is the one that allows an external sensory impression to become transformed into an internal, personally meaningful one. Obviously, such a transformation requires the intimate participation of the emotional or feeling brain.

To See with Feeling

Among the first to link the visual sense with psychic feeling was a researcher by the name of Paul MacLean (1973). MacLean was interested in our evolving capacity for empathy and foresight—the capacity to see with feeling—into others, into ourselves, into the future. The capacity to see with feeling, reasoned MacLean, required a definite link between the visual and the emotional systems of the brain and the newest structure to be added to the mammalian brain during the course of evolution—*the prefrontal cortex*. In humans and higher mammals, the prefrontal cortex is the seat of planning and forethought—the ability to *anticipate* the consequences of our actions before they are expressed in behavior. MacLean and his co-workers were able to trace the connecting pathways linking these brain systems together. This discovery was based on his research on the social greeting displays of squirrel monkeys. These displays, triggered largely by the sight of another monkey, are used in aggressive ways—to show social dominance—but also for mating rituals.

The notion that monkeys and other non-human mammals have the capacity to see with feeling is more widely accepted by the scientific community now than it was in the not so distant past where it was often ridiculed. Serious scientists who dared assert the idea were said to be anthropomorphizing—attributing human traits to animals, a gargantuan faux pas in the world of academia. Thankfully, this antiquated attitude has slowly been replaced by a more fitting one, one that is more in keeping with the facts. For one thing, we now know that the brain systems underlying the processing of psychic pain and psychic pleasure are shared by all mammals. For another, we know that the prefrontal cortex—although it is found in its most highly evolved form in humans—is also present in higher primates where it underlies analogous capacities for foresight and planning.

So why have scientists taken so long to accept the notion the mammals can feel emotional pleasure and pain, that they can demonstrate empathy? One likely possibility is that, in the world of science, ideas frequently have to be proven in the statistical sense before they are accepted as valid. This means that they must quantifiable and measurable. Emotion is difficult enough to quantify in humans and even more so in other species. Even so, can this penchant for measurement account for all the resistance? We certainly found it easy to accept other shared capacities once the common structures were identified. So why did it take it so long to accept this one? Maybe it's because to do so would take us one step closer to accepting our true place in the natural world—as humans yes, but as human animals none the less.

Apart from the world of science where individuals are fee to observe and think and draw their own conclusions—not based on elaborate statistical proof, but on common sense and intuition—this notion probably comes as no surprise, especially to many owners and lovers of pets. Our common experience with our beloved dogs and cats, for example, has done much to inform us. We see it in their eyes, in their demeanors, in their actions. Still there are many humans who lack such awareness. Consider the numerous examples of cruelty and heartless disregard for the feelings of animals still evident in our society and others. On a positive note, there does seem to be more interest in our culture in the emotional life of animals. This growing public awareness, long overdue, that species other than our own have the capacity to form strong emotional bonds and to show compassion both within and across species is evidenced perhaps by the popularity of some of the following books: *Dogs Never Lie About Love* by J. Mason (1997); *When Elephants Weep*: *The Emotional Life of Animals* by J. Masson & S. McCarthy (1995); *The Man Who Listens to Horses* by M. Roberts (1997); *Pack of Two* by C. Knapp (1998).

Binti Jua "Daughter of Sunshine"

A particularly poignant reminder of this capacity was the dramatic rescue of a small child by a female gorilla living at Chicago's Brookfield Zoo (Time Magazine, September 2, 1996). The rescue was recorded on video tape by one of the bystanders and widely publicized in the media. In the late summer of 1996, Binti Jua ("Daughter of Sunshine") was sitting with her daughter, Koola, in the gorilla enclosure when a three-year-old toddler suddenly fell 18 ft. into the enclosure. To the astonished human onlookers, Binti, with her daughter still in tow, went immediately to the toddler's aide, gathering the unconscious youngster gently in her arms and taking him over to the entrance of the enclosure where he was subsequently rescued. Such an act of compassion requires an integration of the visual system with the emotional system of the brain with the motor systems serving as a final common pathway. All of these systems contributed to the final act of compassion with each having a unique contribution to make.

Good Inner Feeling

The type of emotional transformation of sensation revealed by MacLean's work and demonstrated by Binti Jua is pervasive in the human brain. Our every act, our every thought, our every sensory perception is accompanied, to varying degrees, by good or bad feeling. This is simply how the human brain operates and our survival—both physical and psychic—depends upon it. The pleasure we feel inside as we anticipate a favorite meal, see a beautiful painting, put on a comfortable pair of slippers, listen to a favorite piece of music, or receive a warm hug from a friend is possible because of electrochemical activity taking place in the reward system of the brain.

Our understanding of the role of psychic pleasure in human behavior has expanded considerably since the initial discovery of the existence of the brain reward system. We now know that any act, whether in word or deed, that is followed by a feeling of inner pleasure increases the likelihood that the same act (or something very similar) will be repeated in the future. Further, when we are consistently rewarded for something we do or say, we eventually begin to expect a similar outcome before it actually occurs. The closer we come to the final goal, the more anticipatory pleasure we may feel. This good inner feeling motivates us—it keeps us going. It gives us hope and promise allowing us to live through the inevitable frustrations along the way.

The powerful motivating force provided by this system is well known in the scientific community. More recently this understanding has been used to explain, in part, why psychoactive compounds such as cocaine and nicotine and alcohol are so addictive. All of these drugs have been show to have powerful activating effects on the reward system of the brain with the neurotransmitter, dopamine, playing a major role.

Now let's turn our attention to that other powerful motivator, psychic pain.

Bad Inner Feeling

The feeling of psychic pain is as fundamental to human experience as psychic pleasure—perhaps even more so. Within the broader context of human evolution, the punishment system appears to be phylogenetically older than the reward system of the brain. It's not difficult to imagine why nature might have designed it this way. Life was more difficult for the earliest humanoids; as a rule "survival of the fittest" was much more characteristic of their daily existence. In terms of individual survival, the capacity to learn from past mistakes was critical and anything that conferred an advantage would no doubt have been selected for. Put another way, individuals who were good at avoiding harm were more likely to survive until they were mature enough to reproduce and pass on their genes to successive generations.

Psychic pain is a very important teacher much like physical pain. It propels us into action for it is a powerful signal that something is wrong, something that may put our psychic or physical survival in jeopardy.

The phenomenon of psychic pain along with the structures and pathways comprising the mammalian punishment system (also referred to as the periventricular circuit) were first identified by Delgado and colleagues (1954) at around the same time that Olds and Milner (1954) first discovered the reward system. Whenever a pulse of electrical stimulation was delivered to this region of the brain, researchers observed a suppressant or "punishing" effect on behavior. In other words, when animals previously trained to press a bar to receive a pellet of food, received instead a pulse of electrical brain stimulation to this area, their bar-pressing behavior decreased significantly to very low levels. In some instances, depending upon where the electrode was placed within this system, the stimulation was so aversive that the animals never pressed the bar again. This is in marked contrast to the behavior of animals receiving rewarding brain stimulation which was always associated with increased rates of responding, sometimes to the point of exhaustion and even to starvation. In other words, in some parts of the reward system, the stimulation was so intensely pleasurable that it apparently superceded the naturally rewarding effects of food. Animals would starve to death rather than stop the behavior that delivered the rewarding pulse. This is reminiscent of the behavior of addicts who take repeated "hits" of powerfully addictive substances such as cocaine, for example, while ignoring basic needs for food and sleep.

As previously mentioned, scientists now know a great deal about the structures and pathways and neurochemicals underlying the reward system of the brain. The punishment system in comparison has not been as thoroughly studied.

In humans, feelings of psychic pain span the full spectrum from mild feelings of discomfort and annoyance on the one hand, to the more profound feelings of guilt, exasperation and hate on the other. Such feeling exerts a powerful motivating influence on behavior. Whereas inner feelings of pleasure motivate us to do or say or relive in memory those acts that made us feel good inside, inner feelings of psychic pain motivate us to avoid those behaviors or thoughts that make us feel bad. Such avoidance responses are triggered by an anticipatory or expectancy mechanism in the experienced individual.

In other words, when we repeat acts that previously made us feel bad inside, we eventually begin to anticipate a possible reoccurrence of these bad feelings under similar circumstances. Sometimes the magnitude of the feeling is so profound that we bend over backwards to avoid those things that signal, even remotely, a possible reoccurrence. In each case our psychic pain has taught us a very important lesson—we can prevent a restimulation of the bad feeling by avoiding the associated behavior. This is the positive aspect of psychic pain and without it we would be doomed to repeat the same mistakes over and over again. Separate the word bad from the bad inner feeling and all that remains is a cold abstraction—a word without any true meaning.

As we go about our daily activities, the reward and punishment systems of the brain work in a complementary and reciprocal fashion to impart good and bad meaning to our experiences. When the pleasure system is active, the punishment system is suppressed and vice versa. Further, any diminishment in the activity of one system will bring about a complementary increase in the activity of the other. In other words, the formally suppressed system will be freed from its inhibition and go through a brief period of rebound activity. This many explain why we feel so good when we stop banging our heads against the proverbial wall, or so bad when "the party's over". The complementary and reciprocal nature of the relationship between these two motivational systems of the brain was first described by Stein (1964). Stein was also the first to show that rewards and punishments work by an anticipatory or expectancy mechanism in the experienced organism. In other words, *the actual delivery of a reward or a punishment serves a critical, but indirect role in behavior—that of maintaining the expectation.*

Integrating Good and Bad Feeling with Sensory Information

Although we now know that activation of the feeling brain is responsible for our subjective experience of psychic pain and psychic pleasure, we have yet to pinpoint the exact place or places in the brain where psychic feeling and sensory information become integrated into one. One place where feeling information and sensory information come together is in the **thalamus.** The thalamus is comprised of a number of discrete nuclei interconnected with one another. Among other functions, the thalamus serves as an important relay station for sensory and motor information travelling to the highest and outer most regions of the brain. These higher regions are where complex memories are stored, where complex voluntary motor behaviors are initiated and where human capacities for planning and forethought are localized. With few exceptions, all motor and sensory signals arising from the lower brain regions must first go through the thalamus in order to reach these higher cortical areas.

One of the thalamic nuclei, the **dorsomedial nucleus**, is a major stopover for signals relaying emotional rather than sensory or motor information. In fact when contemporary neuroscientists discuss the reward system, the dorsomedial nucleus is often included. Information from this nucleus passes directly to the ***medial prefrontal cortex*** which is also part of the mammalian reward system. The interconnections between the sensory- and motor-specific nuclei of the thalamus and the dorsomedial nucleus make the thalamus a possible site for at least a preliminary type of emotional transformation of sensory information.

In the outer most layers of sensory association cortex and prefrontal cortex, there exists a kind of information-sharing network. This network can be thought of as the place where multiple inputs from the different sensory, motor, and emotional systems converge and "talk" to one another—a kind of neural super information highway and chat room. There is a saying in neuroscience that states: neurons that fire together wire together. Any meaningful coming together or integration of information in this chat room must of course require input from the neurons of the feeling brain.

Plans and Intentions

Information coming from the thalamus is passed on to a region of the brain known as the prefrontal cortex. This is the seat of forethought—of meaningful, goal-directed behavior. It is where plans arise, where one can check on one's progress and where one can postpone or delay the gratification of immediate needs and wants in anticipation of achieving a future goal. This capacity for organized, meaningful, goal-directed behavior is more characteristic of the adult members of our species. It is an outgrowth of our direct experience and its appearance requires cultivation. Exactly when it shows up during the course of development depends upon the interaction between the genetic qualities of the brain and the stimulation forthcoming from the environment as represented by parents and other significant adults in the child's milieu as well as the cultural mores of the society into which the child is born. Young children need to experience the goods and the bads first hand. Only then will they have sufficient experience to be able to anticipate the feeling consequences of their actions *before* they are allowed expression.

There is a saying in the biological sciences that *ontogeny recapitulates phylogeny*. While this is not meant to be taken literally, it means that the development of the individual parallels the development of the species. Consistent with this idea, the maturation of this higher level anticipatory function requires the maturation of the prefrontal cortex, the newest structure to be added to the human brain during the course of evolution, and the last structure to mature during individual development. To see with feeling, to demonstrate compassionate caring and planning for the self and others is the highest form of anticipatory responding. It assures the best possible circumstances for preserving individual and species survival. But its development is not conferred simply because we are human. It must be nourished. One can still think and plan and analyze without feeling. Signals arising in the deeper regions of the feeling brain must be strong enough, so to speak, to traverse the entire pathway leading to the prefrontal regions—to wake it up if you will. If the signals are weak or degrade before they reach their final destination, the human brain will still be capable of thinking and analyzing and planning but without foresight in the truest sense of this word.

Now let's return to the question of temperament and see how all of this relates.

5

What is the Significance of Having a Feeling Brain that is More or Less Responsive Relative to Others?

Opening Comments

It has been our observation that there is considerable natural variability among humans in their ability to imprint feelings of psychic pain and psychic pleasure. Although this may make sense on a purely intellectual level, consider how often we find ourselves surprised and perplexed when confronted by obvious deviations in this capacity, especially when such deviations are expressed in word or deed. It's disturbing when others do not feel as we expect or want them to. How can you be so insensitive we ask? Have you no feeling we exclaim! While giving lip service to the idea of individual differences, we secretly expect conformity. It's as if we were continually asserting the following paradox: I am different from others—certainly not part of the crowd. So why can't everyone be like me? In this chapter we'll explore what it means to have a feeling brain that has a low versus high threshold for the reception of psychic feeling.

The Bell Curve

The innate tendency to imprint the happenings, ideas and people in our lives with deep versus surface meaning can be thought of as opposite poles of the same continuum that shade into one another at some point. Like the colors of the rainbow, this continuum spans the spectrum from the icy blue of no feeling at one pole to the red hot intensity of too much feeling at the other. If we were actually able to measure this capacity in the population as a whole, calculate the mean and other measures of central tendency and then represent the findings in terms of a frequency distribution, the resulting pictograph might take the shape of the Bell Curve, so named because of its characteristic shape. This means that most of us would fall somewhere in the middle of the distribution; that is, we would have an average or "normal" capacity. A small percent of us, however, would fall at either extreme. We would have too much or too little capacity. In terms of the pleasurable component of experience, the problem may lie with the levels of dopamine coursing through our brains at any given time, or with the number of receptors that bind dopamine in the synapse. Too few receptors and the message of pleasure may not get transmitted to our consciousness, too many and we may be overloaded with feeling. But whatever the cause—too much or too little neurotransmitter, too many or too few receptors, a too efficient or a slovenly transport system, the outcome is as follows—for those falling at either pole of the distribution, either too much meaning is attached to an event or too little.

Before we explore the ramifications of this proposed natural distribution for temperament, let's take a brief look at what this means for memory and the internalization of a concept of time in its three dimensions of past, present and future. As we will see, memory and time are important parameters in discriminating one temperament type from the other.

Memory-Feeling Tone Complexes

When an event is processed into memory, so too are the feelings associated with it creating what we have termed a *memory-feeling tone complex*. Memories devoid of such feeling are fundamentally meaningless. They give us little to go on in evaluating happenings in the moment. Such memories are not experiences in the truest sense; rather remain mere recorded happenings, nothing more, nothing less. We have all heard the term "photographic memory" which should help clarify what we mean. The recall of someone with a photographic memory has the accuracy of a still black and white photograph—the memory is detailed, realistic, exact, akin to a series of discrete photo snapshots true to the original event, unbiased by personal feeling. When psychic feeling is added to an event, the memory is transformed into an internally meaningful experience akin to a rich, colorful painting—an external happening reproduced by the senses and emotion of the painter.

When we have a meaningful memory bank of experience, we have something substantive to refer to in determining out behavior in the present. Out of our past pleasures and pains comes a deepening ability to anticipate—to predict the future consequences of our actions based on similar consequences in the past. By learning to avoid situations that signal the potential for psychic pain, we can avoid the actual experience of it. Similarly, by cueing into signals that predict psychic pleasure, we can maximize life's joys. Knowing what makes us happy, what makes us feel good inside, we can point ourselves in a direction anticipated to bring us more of the same. This capacity for anticipating the psychic consequences of our actions is acquired over time under the *guiding tutelage of the feeling brain*.

As we grow and mature, we slowly accumulate a rich memory bank of personal experience richly colored, more or less, with meaning by the feeling brain. This repository serves a very important purpose in terms of the direction our lives take and the choices we make. It is our inner compass—pushing and pulling us in particular directions—closer, hopefully, to those things that forecast the potential for reward; father away from those that forecast the potential for punishment. When this inner compass is functioning normally, we see an individual who is organized in time and in behavior. This individual can relate past to future and thus determine behavior in the present.

Now let's suppose that our inner compass isn't working properly. What would happen to our ability to navigate: At one extreme we might find ourselves chronically adrift in a sea of relentless, meaningless distractions—pushed and pulled this way and that with no rudder to guide our ship. At the other extreme, we might find ourselves stuck in a quagmire of overwhelming meaning, totally unable to move. Of course we're speaking of the two extreme polarities of psychic imprinting here, but even the healthy moderates of the world can be pulled off course by a significant life event—one that produces a more intense activation of the feeling brain for an extended period. If we were to suddenly lose a love one, for example, we might feel lost and disoriented for a time, weighed down by the heavy burden of grief. On the other hand, some event might be so loaded with good inner feeling that is propels us, without reservation, into uncharted waters. If we were suddenly overcome by the beauty of a Renoir or a Monet, we might be temporarily unable to speak. Perhaps the feeling would be so deeply moving that we would decide to change directions completely—becoming an impressionist painter or an avid collector of impressionist art. Such unexpected reactions to external happenings can be viewed as clues that can help us unlock hidden potentials and point us in a more fitting direction—one that is more in harmony with our true inner selves.

The Two Basic Temperaments

We have proposed the existence of two basic temperaments that arise out of natural variations in psychic imprinting. The two types are polar opposites; what exists in one, is absent in the other. One tends to feel in traces, the other, deeply. One tends to live in the world of the immediate moment, the other in the past and the future. One is more lively and extroverted in demeanor, the other, more quiet and introverted. As we will see, the deep imprinters by nature develop a very different view of the world than the surface imprinters.

These polar perspectives represent opposite side of the coin. To have the complete picture, you must be able to see the world from both sides—not an easy feat. You must be willing to work hard and to keep an open mind.

For the sake of clarification, we will describe these two perspectives in a manner that allows the fundamental distinctions between the two temperaments to stand out in bold relief, but variations in imprinting do exist both between and within these two and this should be kept in mind when you consider the following descriptions.

Do-ing and Be-ing

We call one of these perspectives Do-ing and other, Be-ing. At one pole we would have the extreme Do-er type within whom even mild or liminal stimulation of the reward and punishment systems leads to their full-blown activation resulting in the attachment of too much meaning to an event. This is the key that unlocks the understanding of the Do-er. Events and their associated stimuli are deeply imprinted with meaning leading to a weighty experiential past. And when the past is so deeply imprinted with meaning, it weighs heavily in determining behavior in the present. Ever mindful of past pleasures and pains, there is a greater need to test the waters in anticipation of the potential feeling consequences of behavior resulting in an overly cautious, more introspective approach to life. In terms of time perspective, we would say that the Do-er is predominantly past- and future-oriented for the present is always evaluated through the veil of past happenings and future expectations. If the Do-er's past was predominantly negative, his or her future outlook would be one of pessimism. Conversely, if the past was predominantly positive, the future would look rosy.

On the surface, the Do-er appears quiet and shy. But this calm exterior belies the deeper currents within. Strongly bound to an inner world of memories, ideas, and fantasies glued together by strong feeling, the Do-er is a deep individual whose surface waters lie still. To others, the Do-er may appear to be "doing" nothing, but this isn't so. Ways to solve problems and achieve goals tend to be planned and worked out in the mind well before they are carried out in reality. Depending upon the personal meaningfulness of the task, such internal machinations may go on for a considerable period of time before a final path is chosen. A safe assumption, therefore, is that the mind of the Do-er is always occupied. This weighty internal life confers a certain advantage with respect to being able to tune out any distractions. Immediate stimuli, irrelevant to the task, may pass the senses unnoticed leading others to conclude, often erroneously, that he or she has a very narrow view. Getting the attention of one so occupied can be like "pulling teeth". This weight of meaning also imparts a characteristic slowness to the daily rhythm of the Do-er.

Keenly aware of the feelings emanating from others, the Do-er is naturally empathic. In the social arena, the Do-er is at an advantage for she or he can use this sensitivity to tune in to the more subtle expressions of approval and disapproval coming from others, and thus modify their behavior accordingly. The Do-er's low threshold for feeling and empathic nature is evident very early in childhood. This may be observed in infancy as he or she easily succumbs to the soothing voice of the parent, but may withdraw when approached with uncomfortable feelings expressed by others in the immediate environment. The Do-er child is more likely to be labeled the good child, the easy to manage child. Acutely aware of the positive and negative feelings of the parent, he or she quickly learns to moderate their behavior, easily conforming to the expectations of parents through sensing them at a non-verbal level. Here a severe look is sufficient to inhibit the child's non-acceptable behavior while an encouraging smile will drive the child to a further action to please.

As the child's behavioral experiences are labeled good and bad, the first stages of morality are established and behavior becomes predictable. Morality is derived from the Latin word mores which means custom and is related to the rights and wrongs of behavior within a particular culture. The rights and wrongs, the goods and bads are easily acquired by the Do-er as he or she becomes a responsible child early in life. This constant input of feelings, both good and bad, creates a large storehouse of past experiences and forces an internal orientation toward life. It is through their own uniquely, personal past that they view the world. Most typically, the Do-er consults only with him- or herself while evaluating new external stimuli.

As previously stated, the Do-er's perspective is largely past and future. Here future plans and contingencies, once established, become logged into the Do-er's program. Any unexpected changes require heavy mental labor and are not to be taken lightly. Immediate changes must be made in the program which may make him or her both disappointed and irritable. As can be appreciated, surprises are not for the Do-er.

At the opposite pole, we find the Be-er type within whom even strong stimulation of the feeling brain leads to little or no attachment of good or bad feeling to behavior. When the past is devoid of, or only surfacely colored with meaning, it has little or no influence on behavior in the present. Instead of the usual internal conceptualization of time in its three dimensions of past, present and future, a more horizontal conceptualization develops. Here time is experienced as a series of infinite presents—a bunch of discrete happenings unrelated to the past or the future.

When the past and future exist only in the here-and-now, one is apt to be very impatient. Energies can be drained to the point of exhaustion as tasks must be completed *now*; needs and wants must be met *now;* future goals must be achieved *now.* Unlike the Do-er, the Be-er has little appreciation for a slow-persistence-over-time approach to goal achievement. If it can't be accomplished in the here-and-now, the Be-er may give up in despair. At first glance, the Be-er may appear to be very busy indeed—rushing here and there, getting all kinds of things done. But this exterior hustle and bustle is often misleading. Because of a natural tendency to be distracted by stimuli reaching the brain at any given moment, task completion may suffer.

With a less meaningful inner life, one can see how the Be-er's attention would be drawn to and by the external sensory world for the need for direct experience would be much greater. Put another way, the inner feeling of psychic pain and psychic pleasure would be more in the doing and not in the anticipation because external and internal cures would not have their usual predictive value. In comparison to our Do-er type, there is no heavy burden of meaning weighing our Be-er down. This lack of emotional weight manifests itself in a livelier, more energetic demeanor. It imparts a certain quickness and spontaneity to their daily rhythm and actions. This quickness exists in part because there is less of a need to check within in terms of past mistakes and potential consequences. The pure Be-er is an open book—what is on the mind is on the tongue.

It we were of this temperament, we would have been more difficult to discipline as youngsters for in order to internalize parental dos and don'ts we would have had to experience the consequences of our actions repeatedly. While we might have been able to remember what the rules were on a purely cognitive level, the praises and admonishments of our parents and teachers would not have been complexed with sufficient meaning and so would have given us little to go on in terms of direction and self-control. The words good and bad would not have carried the same meaning for us. We would have been perceived as self-centered and strong-willed compared to our sibling with the complementary temperament. We would have been tireless and persistent when it came to getting our own way, but oppositional and defiant when performing at the request of authority. We would have been curious and active youngsters who could be charming and fun to be with when our immediate needs and wants were satisfied.

Feeling Needs and Psychic Satiety

*Now here is an important point—**if one has an easily stimulated feeling brain, one is more easily satiated with respect to the feelings emanating from others.*** This seemingly simple statement has far reaching implications. For example, the Do-er's feeling antenna extend quite far—even to the point of picking up the feelings of others not in their immediate vicinity. Now by this we don't mean a telepathic type of sensing from miles away, rather sensing the feelings emanating from someone in an adjoining room for example. In some cases, this can be quite uncomfortable, especially if the feelings are negative in nature. One consequence of this heightened sensitivity is a greater need for privacy, a greater need for something commonly referred to as personal space or the *buffer zone*. The Do-er requires a wide buffer zone in both their private and public lives as it allows needed time for thinking and for shedding any overload of feeling.

Another consequence of having an easily activated feeling brain is a greater need for emotional coolness in the social arena. This can be better understood if one considers the inner emotional life of the Do-er. With an easily stimulated feeling brain, the Do-er lives in a kind of perpetual internal hothouse. As such, the emotional coolness found in more formal social settings, e.g., the workplace, where there is more predictability and where staid habits of behavior and dress predominate, may come as a welcome relief. Now this shouldn't be confused with the inner intimate would of couple relating. Here the Do-er can be quite close after careful selection of a mate. But even then, the Do-er will need to withdraw from the banquet of intimacy from time to time.

Now let's consider the feeling needs of the complementary Be-er type whose feeling brain is harder to stimulate. Compared to the Do-er, the inner emotional life of the Be-er is on the cool side.

In terms of psychic satiety, it may be said of the extreme Be-er that he or she is *never able to have enough*. This cooler inner life leads to a greater need for feeling attention from others. Consequently, the Be-er's privacy and personal space requirements are less. Being physically alone or even alone in the more contemplative sense, is anathema for Be-ers. Be-ers can tolerate this kind of emotional isolation from others for only short periods, and even then it may cause them considerable discomfort. This discomfort is related to the greater difficulty Be-ers have in keeping the feelings associated with significant others *with* them when the other is physically absent. In the extreme type, only an inner sense of emptiness remains when the other departs. This feeling is akin to free-floating in the universe without a tether—a frightening feeling indeed. In this sense, the Do-er may be said to ground the Be-er.

Even in the more formal social arenas, Be-ers tend to be up close and personal. This arises out of a greater need to experience, directly, the warmth of human feeling. Activities and people and environments that offer greater opportunities for feeling stimulation are highly prized by the Be-er as the feeling emanating from others can help to stimulate the Be-er's feeling brain. Our Be-er seeks open and direct expressions of feeling as more subtle expressions are apt not to register. If the Be-er is extreme, and positive feeling is not forthcoming, the Be-er many push the other for negative attention. Considering the more usual state of the Be-er's internal life, bad feeling is better than no feeling.

Obviously, the characteristics described above may be present in one individual to a greater or lesser degree. As previously mentioned, in an effort to discriminate clearly between the two basic temperaments, traits have often been described in terms of extremes. Again there is considerable variability within the two types. Let's not forget the moderates of the world—those in the golden middle of the continuum, so to speak, where behavior is healthy and adaptive. It is only at the extreme poles that we begin to see psychic illness. Consider the pure psychopath at one pole, for example, with little or no feeling for others versus the pure paranoid at the other who sees meaning and intention where none exists.

A word about how we arrived at the terms Be-er and Do-er: over the years we have tried, unsuccessfully, to come up with better terms but nothing more suitable ever came to mind. To our way of thinking, the term Be-er fit the bill for those individuals who tended to live in the world of the immediate moment, whereas the term Do-er seemed to suit those who have a more active inner life.

The Feeling Machine

Before moving onto the next chapter where we will take a more in depth look at how the two temperaments manifest themselves in real life, we want to introduce you to the concept of the feeling machine as an alternative way of conceptualizing psychic imprinting. Use of the word machine, we felt, would help place the emphasis more squarely on the *automatic* nature of the process.

In this conceptualization, the reward and punishment systems of the brain can be thought of as reciprocally active, complementary, and interdependent parts of the machine producing an ink-like stamping of experience with good or bad feeling. When one part of the machine is active, the other is suppressed and vice versa. Put simply, one can't feel both good and bad at the exact same time. Although we may have bitter-sweet memories, for example, the bitter aspects enter our consciousness at one moment and the sweet at another. Similarly, if we were to suddenly turn down the volume in the bad part of the machine, the good part would go through a brief period of rebound activity before returning to its more usual baseline or background mode.

Essential components of this feeling machine are the ink and the inkpad. The inkpad in this analogy has absorbent properties and speaks to the idea of receptivity. Here we are asking the question: Just how easy is it to turn on the feeling machine in the first place? Do we need a strong and powerful stimulus in order to leave an emotional imprint behind or would a mild one do the trick? The ink in this analogy is psychic feeling. Just as the inkpad may be more or less saturated with ink, individuals may be more of less saturated with good and bad feeling. Put too much ink in the machine, and you may obscure much of the surface detail; put too little and you may not get a lasting, meaningful impression.

The deep imprinter is, of course, our Do-er type as previously described. It doesn't take much to get the Do-er's feeling machine going. Having much absorbent property, the Do-er tends to be loaded with ink. This excess of feeling can cloud the Do-er's perception of events as they happen in the moment. When this tendency is taken to the extreme we would say that he or she has lost all contact with reality, or in keeping with the current analogy, we could say that the ink in the machine "hath runneth over"—that it has spread this way and that, and thus has distorted the perception by obliterating the facts.

Our surface imprinter, on the other hand, is our Be-er type as previously defined and it takes a good deal more, relative to the Do-er, to get the Be-er's feeling machine going. Having less absorbent property, the Be-er is only lightly inked. Less bound to an inner life of deep meaning, the Be-er's senses are wide awake to what's going on in the world around them. When external happenings are processed into memory, there is little ink to cloud the Be-er's perception which means that such memories tend to retain their objective, surface clarity. Who was present, the exact words used, the expression on each of the faces of the participants, what he or she was wearing when it happened, et cetera—all of the superficial sensory facts tend to be accurately recorded and emphasized in the retelling along with their literal or more face value meanings. In this sense, the Be-er makes a good witness. 'He (or she) doesn't miss a trick' is a phrase we have often heard from the parents of Be-er children.

In summary, our temperament is a reflection of the genetic architecture of the feeling brain—the basic wiring that serves to impart meaning to the events, ideas, and people in our lives. And although this function is conferred in large measure by heredity, it may be modified over the course of our lifetime by the environment as well as by certain psychotropic medications, e.g., Ritalin, that alter the neurochemistry and therefore the functioning of those brain structures involved. Some of these medications enhance the imprinting of psychic feeling while others dampen it.

6

Be-ing and Do-ing in Everyday Life

Opening Comments

When people first learn about Be-ers and Do-ers they invariably try to peg themselves as one or the other while putting a value on one type of imprinting versus the other. Often Be-ers see themselves as Do-ers and vice versa. But there is no inherent right or wrong in being a deep versus a surface imprinter by nature. We are, each of us, simply born into the world one type or the other. Each temperament has its advantages and disadvantages and no value judgments are necessary relative to their inherent goodness. In nature polar opposites attract, like positive and negative charges, and in so doing achieve a relative state of homeostasis or balance. We have found these same simple natural laws of attraction and homeostasis to be at work in the realm of human relationships as these polar temperaments find themselves inextricably drawn together in the drive toward personal growth, harmony and completion. When these opposing and complementary perspectives are combined—either through the formation of a couple or through the efforts of one individual over time, they form a stable whole. The process by which one individual develops the ability to look at the world from both sides is termed ***integrating the complement*** and it is difficult work indeed—akin to existing in two parallel and equally real universes at one and the same time.

To further distinguish between Be-ers and Do-ers as they manifest themselves in everyday life, let's compare them in terms of the following:

Fitting

Recall that fitting is one of the basic qualities of feeling as described in Chapter 3. Recall that we said questions always push the mind for fitting answers, that fitting answers make us feel comfortable inside, and that they are essentially idiosyncratic for only the individual can tell *if the shoe fits*.

For the Be-er whose sensory modalities are more keenly attuned to the external sensory world, evaluations regarding the fitness of things tend to be made more on a concrete, pragmatic basis in comparison to the Do-er whose orientation is more inward. Moreover, because the Be-er is less able to weigh the pros and cons in terms of past and future consequences, such evaluations tend to be arrived at more quickly and easily, relatively speaking. In this sense, it's as if the Be-er is a specialist in parallel processing meaning that all of the sensory information seems to be integrated simultaneously into a complete whole. Often the Be-er will be unable to relate, in logical fashion, how he or she arrived at a particular outcome. This seemingly irrational bent can be very annoying to their Do-er counterparts who are either in awe of the quickness of the Be-er's deliberations, or view the process with condescension. We have seen many a Be-e react in anger and frustration when pressed for a logical explanation. Either they don't see the need for one and become annoyed at being questioned, or they may try to come up with one, but can't. Frustrated by their own inability to translate a nonverbal, right-brain kind of instantaneous, simultaneous perception into a left-brain logical, serial one, and sensing a lack of acceptance on the part of the listener, they may react with anger or avoidance.

In contrast to the Be-er, serial processing is the Do-er's forte. For the serial processor time is key, for there is much to take into consideration—one has to go slowly, gather all the facts and proceed in logical fashion from point A to point B and onto one's final point D. Moreover, because the perspective of the Do-er is more internal in nature, decisions regarding the fitness of things tend to be made more in the abstract. By its very nature, abstraction tends to remove one from the reality of the situation to a contemplation of ideals and perfections—a slow process indeed. Depending upon the importance of the decision in the Do-er's mind, a protracted period may be required so that all possible choices and outcomes may be given due consideration. To the exasperation of the Be-er, who isn't aware of the forces driving the Do-er's behavior, the process can seem interminable, so much so that the Be-er is left with the impression that the Do-er will never make a decision. In this case the Be-er may intercede before the Do-er has a chance to act, setting the stage for an inevitable argument.

The Buffer Zone

Switzerland, located high in the Alps where it is surrounded by mountains which buffer and protect the country from intrusion by the warring nations of Europe, is analogous to the Do-er who creates a wide buffer zone between the self and others. This is clearly seen in the group situation where the Do-er is likely to be found on the periphery, at least initially. From the safety of this vantage point, the Do-er can assess whether it is safe to enter and participate. Do-ers are not intrusive and prefer to keep a safe distance from others. With their greater sensitivity to and awareness of the feelings emanating from others, they have a strong need to test the waters in terms of the mood of the group, the receptivity of individual members, the degree of comfort felt. Upon entering a group, attempts are made to be pleasant, but behavior remains cool and formal. Should any unpleasantness be sensed, the Do-er can quietly retreat to search for a more fitting and congenial gathering. In the social arena, particularly if it is an unfamiliar one, caution is paramount.

Unwelcome attempts to intrude upon the buffer zone of the Do-er are typically met with avoidance. If escape is not possible, the intruder many be greeted with cold, forbidding irritation and under extreme conditions, even physical aggression. A dramatic example of this, taken from the psychiatric literature, is presented below:

> Upon reports of physical violence between prisoners in a penitentiary, a psychiatrist was consulted. In an effort to understand the problems of the inmates involved, the psychiatrist devised an insightful and unique experiment. A chair was placed in the center of an empty room. Each inmate in turn was asked to sit in the chair with the request to stop the doctor as he approached from the door at the first feeling of discomfort. Although some of the prisoners allowed the psychiatrist to come very close, even to the point of placing his hand on their shoulders, others halted the doctor when he was several feet away. Upon analysis, it was revealed that the latter groups of prisoners were the initiators of the fights. These men subsequently admitted that they were unable to tolerate the physical closeness of others for prolonged periods—a condition which is standard in the crowded environments of most jails. In fact fighting often resulted in a period of solitary confinement which provided some needed privacy.

Although the above situation is atypical in that there was virtually no relief from the watchful eye and ear of others, it does speak to the condition of the Do-er who requires some degree of privacy even from family members and those few close friends allowed into their immediate world. It is not unusual, for example, for family members to find the Do-er sitting alone deep in thought or reverie or engaged in some solitary activity from which they are excluded. The need to be alone—to have some time to think things through, to review the past and to plan ahead, to shed any overload of feeling—is essential to the Do-er's sense of well being and emotional health yet it is often misunderstood by family members who many take it as a personal rejection.

For the more extroverted Be-er, who is less aware of others on a deep feeling level and whose inner emotional life tends to be on the cooler side, the presence and physical closeness of others is highly prized resulting in a narrow buffer zone, relative to the Do-er, and less need for privacy. The milieu of a party is especially appealing. Craving the feeling attention of others, the Be-er is often found at the center of the group as this position affords the greatest opportunity to extract feeling responses from others. Although not meaning to, the Be-er will often display a tendency to monopolize the conversation and center stage for the desire to be noticed and heard is strong. Without this type of external stimulation, the Be-er is apt to feel empty and alone. Often, if positive feeling responses are not forthcoming, the Be-er may push family members and others with annoying behavior in order to extract a feeling response. The forces motivating this need for physical closeness and direct, open expressions of feeling are not well understood by either the Be-er, who many demand that these needs be satisfied in the here-and-now, or by family members who are unable to respond in a timely fashion.

It is only after much discussion and patience of the part of all concerned that these behaviors can be understood for what they truly represent. Most often, however, mutual misunderstandings and frustrations lead to heated arguments with a recurring theme in which the Be-er accuses the Do-er of being insensitive, distant and uncommunicative, and the Do-er accuses the Be-er of being demanding, controlling, and irrational.

In summary then, we have the heavily-inked Do-er, in whom empathy, caution, and the need for privacy produce a wide buffer zone, creating distance from others pending personal evaluations of them as to the harmony of future possible relationships. This is in sharp contrast to our lightly-inked Be-er whose cooler inner life produces a much narrower buffer zone, less need for privacy, less discrimination in terms of the selection of friends and acquaintances plus a strong need to seek the limelight in search of feeling responses from others.

Bonding

Previously we said that bonding is the "super glue" of psychic feeling—that invisible force that ties people, events and ideas together over time. Bonding has its origins in the imprinting process which, as previously noted, is light in Be-ers and heavy in Do-ers. Our lightly-inked Be-er will tend to form and break ties more easily relative to our heavily-inked Do-er.

Driven by a cooler inner life, the Be-er feels more internal pressure to enter the social arena where he or she may have many acquaintances and friends. The tendency here, however, is to be less discriminating (or more egalitarian) in their selections. Also, because such bonds are not as strongly cemented by deep feeling, they can be broken more easily, relatively speaking. In general Be-ers find it much easier to put the past behind them even after investing a good deal of time and energy in a particular relationship. This may sound heartless to some, but in the Be-er's mind it's just a matter of objective reality minus the emotional coloration or overlay. This is in stark contrast to our cautious Do-er who commits slowly over time and then disengages with considerable difficulty and pain.

The natural cautiousness of the Do-er is seen in all areas of functioning and this is especially true in the context of love and friendship where the Do-er is very selective. Although the Do-er may have many acquaintances, they have few close friends. The bonds of friendship and love are formed slowly as there is a great need to test the waters over time. Once formed, however, such bonds tend to be strong and enduring. In general, Do-ers make loyal and faithful friends. In terms of sharing feelings and confidences however, Do-ers still tend to keep their own counsel. Even within the context of a marriage, the significant other is seldom privy to much of the Do-er's past experiences and feelings. In contrast to the Be-er who experiences much internal pressure to express whatever he or she is feeling or thinking at the moment, the Do-er experiences little internal pressure to reveal their inner most thoughts and feelings. When asked how they feel at any given moment, the Do-er is apt to feel put on the spot. If given insufficient time to respond, the Do-er may withdraw as there is a strong need to think first before answering. This is frustrating for the Be-er who is quick, open and direct in communication. But let's table this discussion on the differences in communication styles until a later section when we get into the topic of the marriage relationship.

Many would be surprised to learn that a Do-er may be strongly bound to a person without ever discussing their innermost feelings. On those rare occasions when they do give vent to their inner world, the recipient may be so over whelmed by the feeling that is emanating that they become immobilized or attempt to retreat either by physically removing themselves or by emotional denial. *I didn't know it was so hot in there* is the position of the Be-er who may be easily overwhelmed by expressions of strong feeling coming from the Do-er even though they need and desire and even push for such feeling responses. We have seen many a Be-er beat a hasty retreat when their Do-er partner finally begins to openly express their deepest feelings even when such expressions are positive. When we inquired about this, many were unable to give a rational explanation rather stated that the prevailing feeling was one of fear accompanied by a pressing need to flee. Our thinking about this is twofold: one, the Be-er is unaccustomed to such depth of feeling and so may be frightened by its expression in others, and two, because its effects are experienced in the immediate moment, the Be-er is easily overwhelmed. So our tongue-in-cheek advice to all you Be-ers out there is to always keep your car in good running condition and plenty of cash on hand for those quick getaways. Obviously, we're attempting to make light of a serious situation that is no joking matter either for the Be-er who doesn't understand why they feel the way they do, or for the Do-er who is equally perplexed by the Be-er's reaction.

A Special Case: The Sudden Bonding of Infatuation

This is a special case of bonding involving the largely subconscious attractive forces at work between the two complementary temperaments as exemplified by the state of infatuation.

Falling in love is surely one of life's greatest pleasures. For a time all seems right in the universe. Joy radiates from every pore; we feel whole and wonderfully distracted, confident that we have finally found the one person meant just for us. Here even the use of the word falling gets at the underlying loss of control that the couple experiences. This is the process of infatuation and it is purely intuitive and subconscious in nature. In Latin the world fatuous means foolish or stupid which is fitting in the sense that during this time no amount of reason by well-intentioned parents or friends can prevent the relationship from running its course. During this time the rational mind is asleep and irrationality prevails. This natural recognition of one's complement can be immediate and profound. In this instance our naturally reserved Do-er, who, as a rule, waits for others to initiate relationships, may take the initiative, but the approach is still peripheral and made with much caution.

Weight

As previously discussed, feelings carry weight. They can be light and buoy us up or heavy and weigh us down. With a heaving imprinting of feeling on events, objects, ideas and people, Do-ers often find themselves bogged down in the muck and mire of heavy feeling. Things can be slow-going indeed for the Do-er during such times when the predominant internal feeling state is negative. Evaluations based on past mistakes result in an expectation of more of the same resulting in a pessimistic attitude toward the future. It is only with much work and rethinking that the Do-er is finally able to extricate him- or herself from the bog. Although an external objective eye might be extremely beneficial during this time, the private Do-er tends *to* work though their difficulties alone without the aid of professional help.

In contrast to the Do-er, the Be-er is less likely to be pressed down by the weight of feeling at any given time. Of course significant life events (e.g. the death of a loved one; the loss of a beloved pet) as well as significant others will always hold greater meaning, but in general the mood of the Be-er tends to be lighter and more tied to current inner impulses and the sensory stimuli of the immediate moment. Reality-bound, the Be-er tends to accept things at face value. Drawn to and by external sensory stimuli, thinking tends to be concrete rather than abstract. For the Be-er, a rose is a rose is a rose. Although the Be-er can appreciate the color, form and fragrance of the rose he or she has little need to embroider it with heavy, personal, symbolic meaning derived from past experiences. While it is true that the rose may trigger other associations, the essence of the rose as something apart from the self with a separate existence is paramount. The rose is a whole unit complete unto itself. Even while viewing the beauty of the rose, the Be-er continues to be apprized of the total immediate environment which the Do-er would tend to shut out as the meaning of the rose was contemplated.

As previously noted the less weighty Be-er has a live-for-the moment, now-or-never, and now-and-always perspective. Demands of the present must be done in the *here-and-now* or the thinking is they will never get done. Expectations must be fulfilled *now*. Goals must be achieved *now*. As such, there is much impatience in the life of this type of Be-er. Although he or she may appear very busy, being less goal-directed relative to the Do-er and more easily distracted, the Be-er may accomplish little. On the other hand, when fully engaged in a task, it may have to be done perfectly since their external sensory orientation makes them acutely aware of any imperfections for which there is little tolerance; such imperfections must be corrected immediately at any price in terms of time or energy. In this case, energies may be expended to the point of exhaustion without the Be-er even realizing it.

In one situation a Be-er wife was informed by her husband that a transfer to another state would be demanded by his work. She was nonplussed and became extremely upset with tears and tantrum behavior, not by the fact of living in another location, but by the act of moving itself which, being unable to see as a series of steps taken each in its time, she saw as an urgent request for immediate action, and was overwhelmed merely by the enormity of the task. She remained obstinate in her refusal to move until the action was laid out to her in a planned series of tasks taken separately in a serially ordered manner. Typical of the Be-er's time orientation, she had brought the future act of moving into the present—something to be done *now*—an overwhelming thought indeed.

The Be-er's life is one or repetitively facing here-and-now situations. Thus when a large task is presented, like the one previously described—one that can be achieved when spread over a series of days or weeks, the responsible Be-er, feeling it must be accomplished now, may appear thunderstruck, become immobile and refuse the task out of hand.

There are some Be-ers who appear to lack any motivation for achievement. In contrast to the responsible Be-er, their behavior appears more random and childlike in quality. They may just hang around, actively doing nothing or, while in the midst of one task, they may lose interest and become distracted by a different set of stimuli which they then temporarily pursue. This type of Be-er tends to rely on others to program their behavior which they may or may not accept depending on existing inclinations. A likely explanation for this lack of motivation is that the reward and punishment areas of the brain are unable to be sufficiently activated with a consequent diminished input from these feeling areas to the prefrontal cortex of the brain which is the seat of self-motivation and planning.

Returning to our original comparisons with regard to the weight of meaning, there is a kind of *unbearable lightness of be-ing* for the Be-er who is ungrounded by the weight of meaning. To find relief, the Be-er seeks refuge in the Do-er who can tether him or her with feeling. Without such grounding, the Be-er is apt to feel totally alone in the universe, cut off from others as if they didn't exist. This is a cold and empty feeling—the cause of tremendous anxiety to the point of panic. At such times relief is sought in the physical presence of a significant other who can provide them with the emotional nurturance they seek. The phone also provides a source of relief for the lonely Be-er who will talk interminably or as long as the listener has the freedom and willingness to converse. The TV is another boon for the Be-er especially those shows replete with heart-rending emotional expressions which can provide temporary relief from a cold and empty internal life.

This lack of emotional weight is associated with a stimulation- or novelty-seeking perspective as well as a greater need for activity. In fact Be-ers often find it difficult to stop moving about. In the extreme Be-er, this hyperactivity appears while still in the mother's womb with random over-activity persisting in infancy and continuing into early childhood and beyond. In such cases, behavior continues its reflexive or impulsive character. In other words, any stimulus, whether internal or external, produces an immediate response with virtually no mediation by the areas of the brain responsible for forethought and self-control.

In addition to the above comparisons, the two basic temperaments can be differentiated in terms of the following:

Communication Styles

The Be-er is direct even to the point of being blunt in communication. Oriented toward the external world, the Be-er approaches others from a surface, reality point of view. Although very perceptive in reading others, the Be-er is unaware of the more subtle nuances of behavior and is impatient to be heard.

The Be-er's speech is clearly enunciated with richness of facial expression and bodily gestures. While seeking to make the point directly there is also much elaboration with imagery in doing so. However, the Be-er may easily and quickly shift gears midstream either because an associated idea comes to mind or a word from the other person sets off a new trend of thought leaving the other in a nonplused situation—completely lost and frustrated. That said, the Be-er may be a joy to listen to and may fire up the listener with his or her oratory.

Conversation between the Be-er and Do-er is a sight to behold. The Be-er, in a clear and often, loud voice, appears to monopolize the discussion. As the Do-er slowly, methodically, and cautiously attempts to make a point, the Be-er who is literally sitting on the edge of the chair and leaning forward, quickly jumps into the discussion at the slightest hesitation on the part of the Do-er, taking the hesitation as a period rather than the intended comma.

In personal communication, the Do-er's approach is indirect and tangential, seldom open and direct. In making a point, the Do-er begins at the periphery while checking the degree of acceptance by the listener. If he or she senses opposition, the Do-er may shift the approach trying to arrive at his or her point through a more acceptable avenue. When acceptance is sensed, the Do-er will move closer to the point they wish to make. Thus the Do-er slowly proceeds, seemingly dancing around his or her point until an open way is found to make it.

In listening, the Do-er is acutely aware of the nuances in the speech of others, tending to read between the lines looking for the underlying meaning of the words of the speaker. In doing so the Do-er will render unto him- or herself their own peculiar interpretation based on their own experiences and understanding of the speaker's attitude toward the issue at hand. The Do-er appears to be a patient listener as they carefully evaluate the tenor and meaning of the spoken word.

Awareness of these two dissimilar and opposing styles in personal communication is essential for any rational discussion between the two temperaments. Such awareness allows the two temperaments to confront each other in a friendly fashion—the Be-er can thereby push for more directness in speech, while the Do-er is freer to call attention to the Be-er's interruptions while attempting to make a point.

Closing Comments

In this chapter we took a closer look at how temperament influences our everyday functioning. Unfortunately, its pervasive influence continues to remain largely unrecognized despite recent advances in scientific knowledge, popular publications, and TV talk shows dealing with the topic.

Once again, while we give lip service to the idea of individual differences we secretly expect others to work like we do. Although this belief may serve us well when it comes to dealing with someone with a similar temperament, it will get us into much difficulty when it comes to dealing with our complement. If we can learn to recognize and understand the basic essence of our complement, we will be in a better position to understand what drives them, what their needs are, how best to live in harmony with them.

7

Meeting in the Inner World of Marriage

Opening Comments

Nowhere are the complementary temperaments more clearly seen in relief than when opposite temperaments are relating in married life. Relationships between opposites require much understanding and acceptance regarding the nature of their polar orientations. In short, it is a relationship that must be worked at with patience and tolerance. The rewards inherent in seeing and learning a new way to oriented yourself to the world are indeed great, as well as necessary, for establishing a more complete and richer identity.

While working with and observing married couples over a long period of time, we observed distinct differences in their style of relating. Initially, we thought these differences were inherent differences in masculine and feminine traits upon which were superimposed differences related to the division of labor and each spouse's predominant concentration of time spent in the outside world of work versus the inside world of hearth and home. However, this assumption helped us only in a superficial way. Something of deeper significance repeatedly disrupted the basic assumptions. Differences were noted in communication style that transcended other differences. Slowly, we discerned two distinct styles which were unrelated to gender or cultural roles—the quickness of the Be-er and the caution of the Do-er. As previously noted, the Be-er communicates in a concrete, direct and practical manner while the Do-er is rationally philosophic and indirect. One of the partners was inevitably outgoing, quick in speech and body movement while the other was laid back, sitting quietly, speaking slowly with measured output with a minimum of body movement as he or she slowly unfolded their reasoning regarding the issue at hand. In fact, these qualities became very evident when seeing the couple together; however, when seen individually the pronounced differences were much less in evidence although they were still observed. Once their temperaments were understood, communication with individual patients was much freer and more meaningful with a subsequent increase in effectiveness in treatment and general understanding. Another dimension of identity was established that took precedence over sexual and cultural determinants.

⌒⦿⌒

Marriage has a number of purposes and meanings. On the cultural level, we have the institution of marriage and all that that implies both legally and socially. In this context, two individuals are joined together in a special kind of mutual economic and social dependence for the purpose of founding and maintaining a family. This cultural-legal definition of marriage carries with it many societal expectations and proscriptions in terms of the various roles that the couple will assume—husband, wife, mother, father, breadwinner, et cetera. With this in mind one would expect the betrothed to think long and hard about matters of heredity, the potential earning power of the other, as well as his or her social abilities and flaws before taking the final plunge. But when the vow of wedlock is made, for all intents and purposes, the rational mind is asleep for there is a more powerful, natural force of attraction operating which renders such matters secondary. Along with the opinions of friends and family, they are mere decorative accents on a much larger fabric of personal meaning. Why should this be so? We advance the answer to be the mutual attraction of opposites in the service of further individual emotional and mental growth.

Making its first appearance in adolescence, this attraction culminates when, through a series of complementary relationships, one finds that complement which best suits one's immediate emotional and intellectual growth needs. It necessarily follows that together the complements are best able to meet life's demands, first as a couple and then later, individually, as each assimilates and integrates the perceptions, values, and abilities of the other. Through the give and take of this relationship, the couple is not only able to meet life's demands, but also to fulfill their initial potentials for growth, many of which were denied while striving to establish a social identity in childhood. Here we are speaking about all of the gender-related habits of behavior and dress that are largely cultural in origin, not about the assigned sex of the individual at the time of his or her birth.

We know that every culture has its particular expectations regarding gender-appropriate behavior. Although western democracies tend to be more liberal in this respect, every culture has its limits beyond which lies certain rejection. To ensure that our children have the best chance of survival, we enculturate them according to custom. The many subtle and explicit ways of communicating what is expected are so ingrained and automatic that we often don't realize what we are doing. Consider, for example, the message conveyed by this Old Mother Goose Rhythm—that little girls are "sugar and spice and everything nice", while little boys are "snips and snails and puppy dog s tails". Such gender-specific tutorials begin very early in life and continue until the child reaches the age of seven or eight. It is at this age, that most cultures expect the child's psychosocial identity to be established. But this important social and developmental achievement carries a hefty price tag, albeit a necessary one, in the sense of adapting to the specific culture in which the child will have to live and compete and survive. To be a girl, one must repress one's masculine side; similarly, to be a boy, one must repress one's feminine side.

After seven or eight years of being all girl or all boy, life, to say the least, can get a little boring.

The feeling here is akin to the way one might feel after achieving a long-term goal. Having finally arrived at the finish line, the question arises, what's next? So when we emerge, at last, from the hood of the child with our gender-specific cloaks firmly in place, the process of looking around for *what we are not* begins. In one sense we are all defined by what we are not. If we are good, we are not bad. If we are fat, we are not thin. If we are bold, we are not timid. During adolescence we begin to search for that missing or repressed side of ourselves in the drive to become whole. This search is aided, in part, by a maturing prefrontal cortex as well as sex-related changes in hormone levels, resulting in a brain that is finally prepared to think on its own. Shades of gray begin to replace the black and white notions of childhood. Things that were once "bad" and prohibited start to look "good" and inviting. The need here is to decide what is good and bad for oneself, not to reject, out of hand, the values of family and culture.

Along with an emerging capacity for independent thought, comes a growing awareness of, and interest in, that which is different. This new-found curiosity occurs on many levels, the most obvious one being the attraction for the opposite sex. Less obvious is the need to find a way to express the many hidden potentialities that were denied us during childhood. The basic idea here is a follows: for every characteristic (e.g., frugality) or trait (e.g., extroversion) that we express on the surface, we could say that the opposing potential lies dormant within us, either in the sense of inborn potential or repressed/subconscious desire. Scratch the surface of that frugal companion of yours, for example, and you might just find an extravagance longing to be free.

By embracing and participating in the world of what we are not then, we can begin to give a voice, either directly or indirectly, to one or more of the many undeveloped potentialities within us. Bold can experience timid by being with timid. Masculine can experience feminine by being with feminine and so forth. Polarities in the natural world and in the world of ideas need one another. They are, in essence, defined by the other. Would heaven exist without hell, predator without prey, extrovert without introvert? One is the complement of the other. Like yin and yang, they are interdependent parts of a complete whole.

The harmonious integration of natural and conceptual polarities is a popular theme in our culture. While easily achieved in fantasy, things are a bit more difficult in real life. When it comes to living, breathing polarities, it takes a lot of hard mental work to achieve unity and balance. This is the difficult work of marriage. And it helps to have an adult brain to do it with—one that possesses such brain-based capacities as insight, open-mindedness, empathy, and patience. Unfortunately, many marriages begin before the adult brain is in place. And even when it is in place, the work is still exacting for differences in the processing of psychic feeling can keep one or both partners bound to their own static view of the world. Learning to embrace a different way of looking at and responding to the world is by no means easy but this is, in essence, what is involved.

Initially, during the honeymoon period, this work may seem easy. With no interference from the outside world, the couple is free to concentrate on enjoying and learning about and from one another. Differences are resolved in an atmosphere of continued infatuation and acceptance setting up the expectation that this is how things will go upon their return to everyday life. Sadly, it is the rare few who are able to retain the qualities of the honeymoon as an integral part of the marriage. Most couples eventually resign themselves to its loss, seeing this as a normal progression in the relationship. And with its loss goes one of the most nourishing aspects of the relationship, for it is through this type of relating that each is able to replenish stores of psychic energy depleted in response to outside demands and expectations. When no effort is made to preserve it, the couple begins to move, imperceptibly at first, away from one another. As the schism widens, the important growth work of marriage comes to a halt. There is a death of former, hopeful expectations. Each partner experiences disappointment and disillusionment.

Many of you may recognize this stagnation in your own marriage. If so, you've probably wondered if you will ever be able to resolve your differences. To this we respond with a hopeful *yes* with the following caveat: as we grow and mature as individuals, the best fitting complement may not be the one that we married. That said, in the ideal world of marriage, our original choice would continue to be our best fit. Now let's explore the five distinct stages of marriage with the understanding that we are essentially talking about a union of opposites.

Infatuation with the Best Suited Complement Available

As previously discussed, the word infatuation bears the connotation of being complacently and inanely foolish and stupid—not something we would openly admit to. But we all know the feeling—the wonderful, extravagant intensity of attraction and pleasure associated with an initial, mutual flowering of love. It is the state of falling in love which implies being overwhelmed by feeling and loss of conscious control. To the couple it appears like they have known each other all their lives which is indeed a part truth for one is a reflection of the suppressed self of the other and represents both the denied gender-identity of childhood as well as the mirror image of the temperament bestowed at birth. During this phase, objective reality is ignored for the most part in the service of maintaining the relationship. Typically it is while in this state of infatuation that wedlock occurs with the pledge of truth and fidelity to one another as the couple departs on their honeymoon.

The Sweetest Month: The Honeymoon

The sweetest month is one of continued infatuation with the connotation that common sense and social dictums, beliefs, and customs are ignored along with their associated pressures and demands. It is a time, so to speak, of social ignorance. A new world is created where nothing exists outside of the couple's relationship to each other. It can be likened to the *Garden of Eden* for it is a world without shame—that painful emotion caused by consciousness of guilt, short comings, and impropriety. In this world, there can be no censures, regrets or reproaches. This is a tender, caring, physical world, a world where instinctual needs can be freely satisfied, a place where emotional energies can be fully restored. Needless to say, perceptions belonging to earlier years that sex is naughty and dirty must be discarded. All is unconditionally accepted and harmony reigns, not despite of differences, but because of the fitting of differences, for the relationship is complementary.

During this time the couple continues the process of knowing one another, not only in the physical, pleasurable, biblical sense, but in the learning of different attitudes, feelings, and ways of thinking and behaving which is perhaps even more important. This willingness to know and understand one another, results in expectations of future personal acceptance. This is the beginning of the benevolent cycle which should persist throughout their lives. Here pleasure and caring beget pleasure and caring which beget further pleasure and caring for each other when responses are open and honest. The openness, honesty and trust that mark this period are essential to the couple's future happiness and must be protected from intrusion by others, even by well-meaning friends and family.

Recall to Reality and Social Expectations

Although the sweetest month must come to an end, the Garden of Eden that was created during the honeymoon phase must be sustained and protected. This is neither a simple nor an easy task for the couple for they have now acquired the labels of husband and wife. These labels have legal and social definitions. Witness the many tombs of law books residing at the state capital which fully delineate the conditions which these roles must fulfill. In this context, marriage is very much a legal and public affair, not simply a license for fornication. At one time the bans of marriage were announced publicly so that others could interfere with the ceremony should any socially important reason be found to do so. Vestiges of this practice can still be found in some of our modern day ceremonies when, for example, the minister asks 'if there is anyone who knows why these two should not be joined in holy matrimony, speak now or forever hold your peace'.

Along with all of the legal dictums regarding these newly acquired roles, there are role definitions given by the class or group to which the couple belongs. And should there be any doubt about what is required, the couple will soon be alerted to their proper performance by neighbors, friends and family members who will be quick to voice their disapproval should they learn of any deviations from expected norms, just as they will be quick to give support when the conditions of these roles are fulfilled. Other husbands and wives will be most willing to share their opinions and experiences about how best to handle an erring partner. To society, the roles of husband and wife are primary and override the significance of the inner, fatuous relationship of the couple which, if exposed or intruded upon, will take on the appearance of mince meat. To maintain the inner world, all doors to the outside world must be shut, for once the attitudes of others or social mores enter, its freedom is destroyed and can no longer exist.

There are so many subtle and not so subtle social pulls and pressures that can take away from the inner, private, restorative world of the couple. Many, like social gatherings of good friends and neighbors, may be welcomed, but require a cautionary note in terms of the degree and nature of the participation. If the gathering is activity-oriented, (e.g., bridge, golfing, dancing), then the focus of attention can be on the game or activity and its intricacies versus the gossipy type of gathering where there may be pressure to reveal intimacies and problems belonging to the inner world. Although it is natural, especially for the partner with the Be-er temperament to be more open in sharing what is on the mind, to do so would, in effect, constitute a violation of this world. And, as we all know, once such private revelations are made public, they tend to take on a life of their own. Moreover, should one's partner learn of the revelation, the foundation of trust which is so essential to the relationship, may be destroyed.

Participation in the male and female counterparts of their group, e.g., the weekly poker game for the husbands, the weekly coffee cloches for the wives, requires this same cautionary note. That said, this separation of the couple can serve an important function as it provides opportunities for continued support for gender identity, especially when it is weak or threatened. It should be noted, however, that gender identity (being a man or a woman) should be well established before marriage, and additionally, that full participation in the inner, fatuous relationship of the couple should allow for a constant reinforcement of same. In this manner gender identity finds its place in the private, intimate world of the couple and no longer needs to be bolstered and supported by traditional social roles. When this is true, there is much more freedom of choice in terms of outside group activities which may be shared as a couple when the same interest is present, or as individuals when the interests differ. Togetherness need not always require the physical presence of the other, which, if overdone, can lead to boredom and stagnation. Each should be free to develop their own individual talents and potentials thereby broadening their interest in each other and the world at large.

Along with the expectations of their social group, the couple must come to terms with the requirements of everyday living: the intricacies of earning, spending, saving and investing; the furnishing, décor, and maintenance of the home; the science of shopping; the art of cooking and cleaning, and so forth. Such functions are typically assigned to the partner with the better expertise, experience and interest, but eventually they can be learned and then shared in the service of fuller individual development and independence which in turn will lead to a fuller inner life together.

At this point we have two complementary, fatuous selves branded with the labels of husband and wife fulfilling the functions of living together in society. But additional social branding is in the offing upon the appearance of the first child.

The Birth of a Child

With the arrival of the firstborn, two new roles are assigned to the couple: mothering and fathering. These roles are also defined and dictated by society which assigns primary importance to the mothering role with particular emphasis on the function of enculturation—the process that insures that the child's attitudes and behavior (morality) will be in accord with the expectations of the group to which it belongs as well as to the larger society in which the group lives. Should the child's behavior deviate from these expectations, it is the mother who will be dutifully informed and woe to her if it is not corrected. Ostracism and excommunication await her if it persists.

Ensuring an acceptable social identity for the child is not easy and requires almost constant parental vigilance especially when the child's territory begins to expand beyond the confines and privacy of home to the surrounding neighborhood. Toward this end, neighborhood gossip and the prevailing attitudes of other mothers will keep her informed regarding the desirability of the child's actions. Additionally, teachers and other school personnel will quickly bring mother up to date not only on the child's academic progress, but on school conduct. Blame and pressure will be brought to bear should the child fail to conform to group standards. Even today, mother is often held wholly accountable for the child's misconduct even if it is, in part, more a reflection of an underlying medical condition such as attention deficit hyperactivity disorder, for example, rather than upbringing.

In the not so distant past, the "good" father was esteemed merely for being a good provider, playing but a minimal role in child rearing—most often that of disciplinarian. It is still within living memory when the last recourse for an unruly child was: "Wait until your father gets home!" In one sense this did work as a disciplinary force for when father finally did arrive home after attending to the frustrations of a long work day expecting to experience the comfort and peace of home, and was faced instead with further tumult, he may indeed have overreacted with irritation and exasperation not only with his child, but with his wife. But as a tool for helping his youngster acquire healthy internal control, it was ineffective for it did little else than activate a sense of fear in the child while adding to the frustration of everyone present.

In the not so distant past and still often today, mothering and fathering were roles assigned to the gender of the parent rather than to the needs of the developing child. Only in recent times has society learned that the genital organs are present merely for procreation and fun whereas the executive, intellectual and feeling areas of the brain are better suited for the complex definition and execution of social roles and innate talents. This more enlightened attitude is slowly working its way into the fabric and structure of modern marriages. Today men can become good primary caretakers and women, good primary providers with no threat to gender identity. Stay-at-home fathers now comfortably take on many mothering functions. Similarly, working mothers now comfortably don professional attire to participate at the highest levels in the cold, formal board rooms of the "dog-eat-dog" world of business. These so-called role reversals are opening the door to further intellectual and emotional growth on the part of both sexes. No longer is gender the deciding factor in determining whether or not one can participate in a social role. Who does the mothering and who does the fathering is now, as it should be, more a matter of the age and the needs of the developing child rather than of the sex of the parent.

Up until the age of puberty, children need a preponderance of mothering. This includes the function of keeping the child alive (fulfilling the child's need for affection and physical sustenance; protection from danger) as well as enculturation. For the child it is basically a time of conformity—of learning what the rules are, of learning to please one's parents and teachers and other significant authority figures. At puberty there is a recall to the inner self. This recall is associated with the hormonal changes of pubescence and the further development and stabilization of the prefrontal areas of the brain—the seat of the highest levels of intellectual activity including such functions as reasoning, planning and forethought. The youth's capacity for independent thought is maturing and it must be respected and encouraged if development is to proceed normally. Among other tasks, it is time for the youth to rethink the early teachings and prejudices of childhood. Some will be retained while others are discarded as they may no longer fit the new self which is emerging. This is where fathering comes in. Fathering is essentially nonjudgmental and non prejudicial. It is a role akin to that of consultant and includes such functions as stimulating the youth's emerging thinking capacities through questions (i.e., the Socratic Method) as well as offering guidance and support in social sexual maturation without attempting to enforce such advice as though it were law. The youth's awareness that it must mediate between its own inner drives and desires and the demands and expectations of society is a challenge for growth to occur as he or she finds acceptable ways of fulfillment within the broader, more complex matrix he or she is now discovering. Moreover, having performed their function of providing a good moral foundation during childhood, parents need not fear this process, for the conscience is in place which means that on-going feedback from the youth's normally functioning feeling brain will ensure that behavior is fitting. Assured of respect for selfhood, the youth will gradually acquire the hood of the adult in a self-confident and self-reliant manner.

The importance of the fathering function to the youth's development cannot be overstated. Sometimes a coach or a mentor can perform this important function, helping the youth become "all that you can be" without harming oneself or anyone else in the process. But how wonderful it would be if this function could be found at home? This longing for fathering is expressed poignantly in the following poem written by a former patient:

DAD

Where on earth
Did our fathers go?
Not the ones today
The good time Joe,
But he who always understood
When you did not know,
Who raised you from a baby,
With still a way to grow.
Is this some kind of magic,
A special place they go?
How he did what he did?
I will never know,
Yet when we could hold our own,
Gently he let go.
I think our eyes on future,
We forgot his special glow.
It makes me warm inside,
He's our dad, and loves us so.

Mutual Self-fulfillment

At this point we have two fatuous complements branded with the social labels of husband and wife, father and mother, living together in society fulfilling the functions of raising and maintaining a family. As previously discussed, this external layering of social roles can interfere with the couple's inner life together. Moreover, in attempting to satisfy traditional role expectations, the two can easily lose sight of their initial vow to one another, whether explicit or implied, of mutual fulfillment. If they are not careful, the necessities of child rearing, earning a living, maintaining a home, et cetera, will take precedence over their fatuous, intimate relating, and before long we will have two individuals living together under the same roof, going through the motions, so to speak, bound together not by choice, but rather by legal and financial and social necessity. This does not have to be. To prevent this stagnation in the relationship, it helps to be aware of some common traps that couples unknowingly get caught up in with the understanding that if one is aware of them, one can take steps to work through them if and when they arise. We've already discussed how the loss of the Garden of Eden can prevent the much needed restoration of psychic energies depleted during the day. Let's see how other factors may conspire to erode the ever longed for state of harmony and mutual fulfillment.

Common Pitfalls:

The Mother Trap

Without realizing it, many women become dedicated mothers to the exclusion of other self interests. One young mother—a highly intelligent woman who was even allowed to skip a grade in high school because of her quick mind and excellent learning abilities—came into our office with complaints of depression and inferiority. For the past two years she had found herself unable to actively and intelligently participate in discussions with her husband and his friends. This period coincided with the birth of her firstborn who was now two years old. It was revealed that upon becoming a mother, she devoted all her energies to caring for her child. Her only social life had consisted of her relationships with other mothers whose conversations were limited to mothering, housework and cooking. With such limitations, her mind was no longer challenged or stimulated resulting in a seeming atrophy of the intellect. As she became aware of the trap she had fallen into, she was able to expand her interests and social activities not only with no detriment to her child, but also with a reawakening to the previously healthy relationship with her husband who admitted to feeling left out and isolated since the birth of their daughter.

Sometimes women get so caught up in this function that they even begin to address their husbands like they address their children. What came to mind in writing this was a TV commercial where we see the husband arriving home at the end of the day and opening the door only to be greeted by his wife who begins speaking to him in baby talk. At this point hubby, perceiving his wife's need for a change in attitude and environment, goes on-line to make a reservation for a romantic evening out. But even this change in venue doesn't have the desired immediate effect as we see his poor wife, now dressed in evening attire, still struggling to shed the hood of mother as the scene draws to a close.

The Five O'clock Crisis

When the inside world of home intersects with the outside world of work for the first time following a long, arduous day for both wife-mother and husband-father, the stage is set for mutual misunderstanding and irritation. To understand the why of this, one needs to have an appreciation for where these two individuals have spent most of their day. For didactic purposes, let's assume that we have the more traditional family structure of the past with wife-mother confined essentially to the inside world of home, and husband-father to the outside world of work. The two worlds are complementary with differing values, interests and priorities. Among other differences, the inside world is a place where "small" things are important—things like dust and trinkets, neighborhood gossip and leftovers. It is a place where only "minor," ordinary everyday things happen. This is in contrast to the outside world where big, major events happen, a place where "large" things are important—things like closing the deal, vying for status and power, outdoing one's peers in order to gain financial and positional advances. Like other complementary values and interests of these two worlds, taken together, they provide us with the complete picture of family life. But therein lies the rub. It's not always easy to understand the differing values and vicissitudes of these two worlds, unless one experiences them directly and routinely. On the other hand, direct experience need not be a prerequisite to understanding if one can trust in the feedback provided by the partner with the greater first-hand knowledge.

As previously noted, until recent times, it was wife-mother who was assigned almost exclusively to the inside world. This world was limited geographically. It included, for the most part, the home, the neighborhood, the grocery store, the school, the doctor's office, the shipping mall, the beauty salon, and the post office. Glimpses of the outside world were provided primarily through the local newspaper, TV, and magazines. Soap operas and talk shows also offered wife-mother an opportunity to experience, vicariously, the emotional turmoil and actions of others, thus opening the door for occasional fantasy and escape. To the inside world, immediacy and intuition are of great importance. As a mother, immediacy of response is essential in protecting the health and needs of little ones who are ignorant of the many dangers that exist both in the home and neighborhood. Proper meal preparation, proper care of leftovers, repeated dusting and vacuuming, proper cleaning of the children and their clothes in preparation for school and other occasions requires an ever vigilant eye. Wife-mother has little time to engage in the slow, deliberate, rational process of thought. When a youngster's actions are inappropriate or many result in physical harm, her response must be immediate. Should she delay to consider the pros and cons of her intrusive behavior, the youngster might well be dead by the time she decides to act. In this sense wife-mother must rely solely on her intuition—an unconscious immediate response resulting in an impulsion of thought and action which gives up the intermediate process of rationalization in favor of a practical and life-preserving outcome. One can see how repeated responding in this manner over time can become a habit which pervades other areas of functioning as wife-mother discovers that her intuition is virtually faultless. However, total reliance and trust on her unconscious processes, although effective in the inside world, may make her appear stupid and inappropriate with the what, and the why, and how come demanded by the outside world. This world has a cold, formal, personally distant atmosphere. It is a world full of constant pressure and tension; a world of social and oftentimes, of physical survival.

In contrast to the outside world, the inside world is warm, emotional, close and responsive. It is a place where the heart and the hearth are open, a place where family members can be free to shed the habits of thinking and dress and behavior that are the mark of functioning in the outside world. But it is also, at times, an emotional and physical hothouse especially for the partner who must spend their entire day within its confines. Routine activities such as cooking and baking and cleaning as well as tending to the physical and emotional needs of young children who are, by virtue of their age, essentially helpless and tethered to her skirt strings can easily heat up wife-mother who may in fact feel overheated and over confined toward the end of the day. Wife-mother may even contemplate a soirée into the coolness of the outside world, or, at the very least, a breath of that world upon the arrival home of husband-father.

On the other hand, husband-father, having spent his entire day in the emotionally distant and cool formality of the workplace, contemplates the warmth and comfort he will receive from his wife and children upon his arrival home, or, at the very least some peace and quietude in order to recover from the day's stresses. Needless to say, the needs of wife-mother are in complete contrast to the needs of husband-father at this point in time. One seeks freedom of movement, a fresh breeze of outside air and distance from the heat of the hearth; the other seeks intimacy and warmth, to be welcomed into the caring, outstretched arms of loved ones with appreciation for the day's battle which has just been waged on their behalf. Guess whose needs will be given priority? Unfortunately, in the past, society, through its various media, has emphasized the importance of the outside world where "big" events take place and new, exciting things happen. The outside person and their role were to be supported at all costs, and therefore, according to custom, their needs came first. At least this was how things went in the conventional marriage relationships of the past and to some extent it still happens today. If the outside world person, whether this is father or mother, can be made aware of this, then he or she can help relieve the situation by, for example, playing with the children for a time giving the inside world person time to finish preparing the evening meal.

Luckily this structure has undergone a dramatic change in the past few decades. A new, freer, more flexible, more functional unit is emerging with a fuller appreciation of the potentials and abilities of the female partner with a corresponding expansion in the growth of the male partner.

Habits and Habitats

By this we mean habits of thinking, dressing and behaving that accompany the performance of a particular social role. They are functions of the self through which some potential or skill may be expressed in the outside world. Habits are also havens—places of safety. One can hide in a habit. But habits can also smother the self. You can get caught in a habit and never get out. We already discussed the mother trap, but this idea applies just as well to the other habits of thinking and dress that people can get caught up in, for example:

Doctor habit
Professor habit
Lawyer habit
Sales person habit
Preacher habit

To the outside world, habits are very important. Whenever we don the habit appropriate to the function, it gives us credibility and signals to others that we know what our role is, that we know what we are doing. Assuming all of the behaviors and thought patterns and codes of dress appropriate to the role, we can usually go about fulfilling our function as expected and required without too much aggravation in terms of the disapproval and questioning that would come, for instance, if we acted or dressed, so to speak, in a manner unbecoming. In this sense, specific habits go with specific habitats. The wisdom of the habit is expressed in the familiar adage 'When in Rome, do as the Romans do'.

Although habits have their place in the outside world, they can get us into difficulty when we try to take them with us into the inside world. One specific example comes to mind—a more traditional husband-father type who was unable to shed his outside uniform at home. Even on the weekends, he was uncomfortable without his white shirt, polished shoes and dress pants. This was true even when he tackled the fixing up and repair of the home. Unfortunately this difficulty extended to habits of thought and attitudes that were more suited to the workplace than to the home. This tendency alienated him from those he cared for the most, limiting his emotional and mental growth. When you use outside social role definitions in the inside world, you cease to be an individual. You become, for example, merely a mechanic and a data processor living together.

Another area where old habits of thought can get in the way of the couple's relationship is in the area of sexual intimacy. To have a full, rich, mutually satisfying intimate life, all manner of thinking that sex is dirty and naughty must be discarded. Hopefully this attitude, left over from childhood, is shed as we don the hood of the adult. For many, however, this is not the case. Traditionally, since biblical times, it has been the female of the species who is viewed as the bad, sinful, dirty temptress—luring the male of the species into thoughts and acts that are "impure". Recall that it was Eve, not Adam, who was responsible for original sin and expulsion from the Garden of Eden. Many cultures still view women in this light, requiring them to cover themselves in public so as not to temp the sexual appetites of males. Vestiges of this anachronistic view survive today even in our culture where, depending upon how she is dressed, a woman may be referred to as a slut, a whore, or a tramp. Comparable terms of derision do not exist for men in our culture. Such habits of thought interfere with a healthy sex life. Some men evidence what psychologists refer to as a Madonna-whore complex. Bluntly speaking they cannot perform in the bedroom with wives who have been placed on a pedestal for these are women who are pure as the Madonna herself and completely untouchable in the biblical sense. Men with this difficulty often feel compelled to seek sexual gratification outside of the relationship, with prostitutes and other women, who, to their way of thinking, are "dirty". One can easily imagine what this does to a couple's relationship. Women have their own anachronistic cross to bear in this arena too. Recall the old fashioned view of sex as a duty, something one must submit to in the interest of fulfilling a wifely function rather than as something to be enjoyed fully and without shame by both partners. Thankfully, we have popular media figures like Dr. Ruth and Dr. Oz who are helping ordinary folk see sex in a more healthy light. In the words of one of her admirers "Dr. Ruth is making sex clean".

Communication

One of the most common complaints of couples is an inability to communicate. "He doesn't listen to me."; "She constantly interrupts."; "I can't make her understand."; "He just tunes me out."; "I say one thing and he thinks I mean something else."; "I can never get a word in edgewise."; "She withdraws when we have an argument." These are among the oft heard complaints. Without realizing it, this is one of the many areas where the two are unwitting victims of their own natures. Recall that we view the marital relationship as a union of opposing, but complementary temperament types. Temperament has profound effects on marital behavior, and the world of communication is no exception. We would go so far as to say that without a fundamental understanding of basic differences in temperament, it is impossible to have a truly fulfilling marriage. Unfortunately, the pervasive influence of temperament is still widely unrecognized despite the renewed interest in the role of nature and genetics in behavior.

Speaking in general terms, like temperaments have an easier time communicating for they intuitively recognize and understand one another. With their acute sensitivity to the feelings emanating from others, for example, two Do-ers can communicate comfortably without having to say a word. It's not unusual to find two Do-ers sitting quietly together in silence, enjoying the peace and quietude as it fills with mutually understood meaning. When Be-ers are together, however, there is apt to be much verbosity and noise for what comes to mind tends to be readily and openly stated—often in dramatic fashion with arms waving and gesturing, face expressive and radiant. One Be-er may interrupt the other with an immediate thought and the other feels no hesitation about doing the same. This tendency to interrupt doesn't seem to bother either of them and the communication between them appears easy and direct. Be-ers relate on more of a horizontal plane in terms of communication—speaking just as openly and directly to the CEO of a company as they do to the janitor.

Communication between a Be-er and a Do-er is much more difficult. The two temperaments simply don't understand each other's style or the forces driving it. As previously noted, Do-ers tend to approach slowly and tangentially. There is a tendency to read between the lines looking for hidden meaning. A Do-er may start off at point A with the hope of reaching their final destination, point D. If A is accepted, they move to point B and so forth. Sensing any negative reaction on the part of the listener, they may retreat to point B; if further negativity is encountered, they may never reach their final point, D. Tact, appreciation of nuances, and avoidance of conflict are paramount in the Do-er's mind. In this sense, a Do-er's communication has a distinct oriental quality—subtle, indirect, and veiled. Said another way, the Do-er tends to speak in a roundabout fashion, getting things out piece meal so that they don't create a disturbance.

Be-ers, on the other hand, are far more direct to the point of being blunt. They say what they mean and mean what they say—at least in the moment. Relatively speaking, the Be-er is not as concerned with the feelings of others, rather more with the facts at hand. Frequently this gets them into trouble as they may unintentionally offend as they proceed to call it like they see it. Be-ers also tend to think out loud and to shift quickly between various topics—what is on the mind is on the tongue aptly describes their style. Be-ers also tend to interpret what is being said on a surface, literal basis. One Be-er patient openly admitted to being confused by the common expression 'see you later'. "I actually thought I was going to *see* them later. It took me a while to understand that this was just another way of saying good bye."

Now I'm a Be-er by nature and I can readily identify with this literal bent. As a young child, I remember vividly the first time I heard the phrase 'read between the lines'. I was fascinated and went immediately upstairs in search of a recent letter from a favorite cousin. With considerable excitement, I began trying to do just that, but all I saw was white, empty space. No matter how hard I concentrated nothing new and deliciously secretive appeared in those empty spaces. I have to laugh at this now, but this tendency caused me considerable confusion during my early years at school. It seemed that I always had to get through the concrete, literal interpretation of an abstract expression before I could get to its underlying meaning. Naturally, the more exposure I had to this "odd" way of thinking, I got better at figuring out what was expected. But it didn't come naturally. It was a struggle that was at times painful for not only did I risk public embarrassment if I couldn't immediately come up with the deeper interpretation, but I also didn't see the need to look here and there and everywhere beyond the surface for some oblique meaning, and I wasn't adverse to saying so to the frustration of many of my teachers. To my young Be-er mind, if it was so important, why not say it clearly and directly in the first place? Although many of my Be-er friends can readily identify with my impatience with such mental gymnastics—from their own personal struggles—this literal bent continues to perplex many Do-ers.

Unfortunately "abstract reasoning" is still touted by many as the quintessential indicator of general intelligence. One has to wonder how many young Be-ers have fared poorly on IQ questions such as "What is the meaning of 'shallow brooks are noisy' or 'still waters run deep' or 'a bird in the hand is worth two in the bush'? I've actually put these questions to some of my adult Be-er patients. To my surprise, many evidenced a continued difficulty in getting past the surface, literal interpretation.

One can easily see the potential for conflict that arises out of these two different communication styles—both in terms of the private world of personal relating, but also in terms of the more formal relationships of the workplace. When communicating with a Do-er, for example, Be-ers must be reminded that pauses in conversation should not be confused with periods. The tendency of the Be-er is to jump in before the Do-er has finished expressing their thoughts and feelings. So our advice to

Be-ers has often been that if they really want to know what is on the Do-er's mind, they must be patient, refrain from interrupting, and learn to be comfortable with what may feel to them like an interminable silence. We have also cautioned Be-ers not to misinterpret a lack of response in the moment as a personal rejection or unwillingness to communicate, rather more as the Do-er's need to have some time to think things through before responding.

With respect to communicating with a Be-er, Do-ers are cautioned to keep in mind that Be-ers have trouble reading between the lines, that they therefore need and value more direct, open expressions of feelings and thoughts, that they tend to think out loud, and moreover, that what is said should be accepted at face value, nothing more, nothing less. In other words, don't keep looking here and there for hidden meaning. In terms of the Be-er's literal bent, I also caution the Do-er to follow through on their promises. If you say you will call later, for example, make sure you do as the Be-er will call you to task if you don't. This is not to say that Do-ers don't intend to keep their word, rather that they have an easier time making allowances for unforeseen circumstances more easily than the Be-er. Whereas the Be-er may be found pacing back and forth, waiting literally all day by the phone, the Do-er, in the same situation, may find it easy to go about the business of the day, putting the anticipated call on the back burner, assured that if the call does not come at the appointed time, that a reasonable explanation will be forthcoming.

One last point needs to be made. Since the tendency of the Be-er is to think out loud, we caution the Do-er to help them think things through without being judgmental or condescending. This will go a long way in establishing mutual respect and open communication.

Acceptance and Trust

Many people think of the private, inner world of a couple purely in terms of sex. Some will throw in the need for communication, but they don't know about, or understand the two basic temperaments, or how to communicate based on that knowledge. Each person has different needs and communication styles, and these have to be known to relate effectively. Here, as in other relationships, we see the same old paradox in operation—paying lip service to the idea that others are different from us but at the same time secretly expecting them to work like we do. So how do we go about overcoming this difficulty in the context of marriage?

The word acceptance comes immediately to mind. Acceptance leads to appreciation and caring. Accept what is part of yourself and it comes under your control. In the same way, when you accept others they become part of you. Accept that differences exist between all people, and then, with the knowledge of differences based on temperament, you will be equipped to see situations, to appreciate the dynamics involved, to know what to expect from your partner and how to respond.

Another word that is preeminent in my mind is trust. To really understand what your partner is all about, you must be willing to yield a fixed point of view. This is scary stuff indeed, for it is a reconsideration of a viewpoint completely opposite to your own, and reciprocity in terms of trust is essential to the process if you are going to allow yourself to be vulnerable in this way. Each partner literally brings something to a given situation that the other doesn't have, so it has enormous potential to be a very enriching experience. To understand and appreciate what that opposite perspective is all about, you must be willing to suspend judgment, to open yourself to a new way of looking at things in order catch a glimpse of a parallel reality of equal validity. Now it's not a case of giving up your own reality, rather more that you are adding on to that reality. When you have trust in your partner, you can let your partner have their way in a given situation. It won't always have to be "my way or the highway". And then, if there is any merit in your partner's way, you can begin to use it for yourself. By making it a part of you, you obtain a fuller, more complete identity. This is the difficult growth work of marriage, achieved sometimes through sheer agony. Each partner needs the heartfelt cooperation of the other for it can take a lifetime and then some to integrate the complement. Throw in a good measure of tolerance and patience, and you have a recipe for success achieved gradually over time.

Unfortunately we have seen very little emotional trust between marriage partners. Most of the time, the only meeting of minds occurs over external things. They can meet over their finances or planning a party, or going to their child's soccer game, but so far as the inner world goes, which is intrinsically the place where they would share their core feelings, perceptions, and experiences, they are not meeting. People are so busy living in the outside world all the time that their inner world suffers. This lack of meaning in the inner world is why loneliness is so rampant. Frequently in our practice, we have heard variations on the following theme: "I want someone I can really be intimate with. I don't mean just going to bed, but someone I can really talk with". To relieve this loneliness, it is critical for each partner to link up with the other at a deeper level. The Do-er will be glad to get out of the morass of heavy feeling and be with the light-hearted Be-er cruising around in the treetops so to speak. And the Be-er will welcome the Do-er's warmth and sense of grounding.

Unfortunately, timing is often a problem for the two. The Be-er will want to talk about something of importance, for example, and the Do-er will be preoccupied with their internal agenda and thus be unable to respond in the moment. Out of frustration and not realizing that the Do-er is preoccupied internally, the Be-er may lash out at the Do-er's apparent disinterest. Now at this point, the Do-er, who is also unaware of the dynamics involved, may simply walk out leaving the Be-er in a further state of exasperation. Later the Do-er may come back with a considered response, but by that time, the Be-er may have already forgotten the issue and, with much incredulity say: "Why are you talking about that now! That happened last week!" Keep in mind that before disclosing their core feelings, the Do-er must think about what will be shared as well as how it will be received. To a Do-er shame and embarrassment are to be avoided at all costs, and that is one reason why total trust from a Do-er is slow in coming. On the other hand, the Be-er will be more open and vulnerable in sharing their feelings and experiences in the moment, but if this is not reciprocated in kind, and, at the same time, the Be-er will grow impatient with and mistrustful of the Do-er.

Trust is fundamental. Without it there can be no true appeasement of inner needs. Actually, in general, I see very little trust socially, although you won't find many people agreeing with me on this point because the consensus is that trust is a very important quality to have and to extend. If someone told you outright that they didn't trust you, you'd feel insecure and offended. You might even want to say goodbye to them.

People do have to be careful who they put their trust in. It is a big investment with inherent risks. If you invest your personal self into someone else and they disappear, it's like losing stock in the stock market. If you believed your financial advisor, for example, and invested all your money into investments that didn't pan out, you'd begin to question your own judgment. Multiple losses of this nature of people you once considered "trusted" friends or lovers or associates can lead to the feeling: "I really am unable to properly evaluate another person". If you can't rely on yourself, who can you rely on? At some point, you become unwilling to take chances. Even if some nice, trustworthy person comes along in the future, you don't dare entrust yourself again.

Why is there such a lack of interpersonal trust? Again, think of what we expect from others. As previously discussed, most of us expect others to work like we do. Suddenly, we discover that they don't. But things might look a little brighter if we all knew about and accepted fundamental differences based on temperament.

Miscellaneous Food for Thought

Before concluding we would like to share with you an observation that may be of some use to couples with children. Specifically, as we began using and refining our perspective on temperament in our clinical practice, we observed that the temperaments seemed to alternate in terms of birth order. In other words, if the first child was a Be-er, the second was invariably a Do-er. This alternating between temperaments held true unless there was a miscarriage or an abortion between births. We don't know why this should be so, but it occurred so consistently that we couldn't ignore it. Perhaps this is nature's way of insuring a balance. Now we don't have any proof to report in terms of statistics so we only ask that you view it as intended—merely an observation pressing enough that it bears further investigation.

The above observation also brings to mind the importance of considering the temperament of the child in terms of parenting. Parenting techniques, out of necessity, need to be tailored to the temperament of the child to be effective. What works with one will not necessarily work with the other. We can't tell you how many times we have heard the following lament: "We raised them both the same, and look how they turned out!" Keeping in mind what we view as the three cardinal backbones of discipline—immediacy, consistency, and constancy—the Be-er child, relative to the Do-er child simply requires more of everything—more immediate feedback in order to help them complex good and bad feeling with their words and deeds; more consistency, i.e., if something is "bad" one day, it can't be "good" the next; more constancy, i.e., more open, unconditional reassurances that he or she is loved and valued and accepted for who they are. Again, this doesn't mean that Do-er children don't need this too, just that Be-er children, because they have more difficulty picking up on and therefore internalizing, the feelings emanating from parents and other significant authority figures, require more open, frequent, consistent, immediate, and concrete expressions of same, in order to be able to internalize socially acceptable ways of modulating their needs and wants within the broader context of family and culture. This approach is especially important when attempting to enculturate a Be-er youngster who is overly active, relative to other children his or her age, and who may be at risk for the development of symptoms collectively referred to as Attention Deficit Hyperactivity Disorder (ADHD).

Because of the almost constant vigilance that many Be-er youngsters require, the needs of a little Do-er sibling can sometimes be neglected. It's not intentional on the part of parents, just that Do-er youngsters tend to be on the quiet end of the spectrum, and, as we all know, it's the squeaky wheel that gets the grease. Parents are therefore cautioned to check in frequently with their little Do-er youngsters—to be with them in the feeling sense—even when they are quiet. This will insure that the little Do-er's needs are being met, and it will also help alleviate any rivalry between siblings in terms of competing for essential parental attention.

There is another observation that also may be of use in terms of parenting. This observation is directly related to the idea that experience or nurture can push genetic constitution around. Specifically, we have noticed that when mothers and infants have opposing temperaments, the fit, overall, is "better" in terms of the flow of psychic energy between the two. If you think, for example, of Be-er children needing more feeling stimulation right from birth, and of Do-er mothers as having perhaps an excess of feeling that can be used to soothe and calm the Be-er child—warming up his or her feeling machine—then, in this sense, the emotional needs of both are well-served by this dynamic. The Do-er mom can get rid of some of the excess by giving it to her Be-er child. In the process mom is "cooled down" while baby is "warmed up". In similar fashion, the overly sensitive Do-er baby or youngster (here again we are referring to the ease with which the feeling brain is stimulated) may be relieved by a more casual, reality-oriented, matter-of-fact Be-er mom. After all, if mother over-reacts with excessive concern or empathy to some minor mishap then the minor mishap might take on excessive emotional significance for the child whose feeling brain is genetically primed to work in over-drive.

In the world of science, this idea of using mother's personality to modify the child's personality has been tried using rhesus monkeys. When infant monkeys, who had been bred to be inhibited and fearful, were given to foster-mother monkeys who had opposite personalities—that is, uninhibited and fearless—not only did the infants become bold like their new mothers, but they also developed the relevant brain neurochemistry, which for the trait of boldness meant low levels of the neurotransmitter, norepinephrine. Most surprising of all, the changes appeared to be permanent. This work was done by Stephen Suomi and colleagues at the National Institute for Child Health and Human Development (Wright, W., 1999, Born That Way: Genes, Behavior, Personality).

Summary

In this chapter we discussed the marriage relationship in the context of temperament and the cultural and social pressures that go hand in hand with having and raising a family. We said that marriage is a relationship of opposites and that one of the underlying forces driving this union is the need for growth, both emotional and mental. We took a look at some of the common pitfalls that get in the way of a mutually satisfying and fulfilling relationship and more importantly, how problems based on differences in temperament can be resolved and utilized for further growth rather than alienation. Although the important growth work of marriage—what we have termed integrating the complement—can easily take a back seat to the necessities of rearing a family and providing for the physical and psychic needs of offspring, it is crucial to the health and stability of the couple. When the growth world is recognized and valued and given its rightful place in the relationship, the union can truly attain the ideal of mutual fulfillment and satisfaction.

Yes marriage is difficult. We all know the statistics—over half will end in divorce; but it has the potential of providing family members with what will be in the best interest of each and all, especially in light of the new structure of marriage which is weaving its way into the fabric of modern American culture. This more enlightened union of fatuous selves does not result in each being branded for life by the external layering of social roles which restricts their emotional and intellectual growth, but rather represents the joining of two complements to form a whole unit through which each may fulfill their innate potentials, first as companionable partners promoting the others growth and second, by independently contributing to society as a whole. Such a union can bring harmony, contentment, and happiness so long as the inner world of the couple is maintained and nourished. When this is lost, the couple will be subject to an unbalanced life of discontentment and illness—physical and/or emotional—as they search, usually in inappropriate ways, to reclaim that most precious commodity which is the source of needed energy and comfort.

8

Closing Thoughts

When I began this work, some time ago now, I wasn't sure where it would take me. I knew I wanted to pay tribute to my friend, colleague, and mentor, Willis H. Ploof, MD, who passed away too soon, long before the world had a chance to know of his contributions to the field. Dr. Ploof was a quiet, private, gentle man, a deeply sensitive and complex man, a thinker and a planner, a Do-er by nature. I also knew I wanted to put into ordinary, everyday language, the perspective on human temperament that had evolved during our time together. It has always been our intention to make it available to the ordinary person, who isn't ordinary by any stretch of the imagination, in the hope that it would help to inform and improve their most significant relationships with family, friends, and loved ones. Together, I think we have accomplished his.

As I reflect now on the entirety of this work, I am filled, as he was, with a feeling of hope—hope for us as humans, hope for our ability to bring ourselves and those we cherish closer to the goal of having an empathic, compassionate, forward thinking society that functions for the good and betterment of all.

Hope is a delicate, ephemeral entity—something glimpsed from the mind's eye that flies free on the delicate wings of human feeling and fantasy. I see now, more than ever, that the means to a better future lies within the brains of our leaders and the brains of ordinary folk like you and me. A mature meeting of mature minds is what is needed. We have it within us to accomplish this goal, but will we? I used to believe that evolution was a forward, advancing kind of process, that the utopia that we all long for would just be a matter of time; as we evolved as a species, we would be better behaving humans. I know now that this view is naïve—that evolution can go backwards as well as forwards. So it seems that it is imperative that we learn as much as we can about our nature so that we can take steps to better our nurture.

In closing I would like to leave you with the unedited words of Dr. Ploof, written a few years before his passing, when the early seeds of this book began to take form. It will give you a flavor of his nature and the benevolent, fatherly attitude he had toward the human species:

"Have an adventure with me over old familiar places of play and life; places that will, alas, seem strange but, once seeing them again will seem like old haunts. All things spoken of in this story, all the experiences, facts, logic, will not be new to you, but maybe seeing them again as part and parcel of one large picture of human existence, will be of some help in relieving the confusion of part truths, self-concealed truths, and paradoxical truths. Let us take the story of human life not only from the human, spiritual, physical viewpoint, but also from the influence which society and civilization, both past and present, have had upon us. To speak with you, I must use words. You must read them. It is important, therefore, that I make my words clear and defined to you—at least the words I feel are most important to convey my thoughts, ideas, observations and knowledge to you. I do not ask you to accept my definitions except only during the reading."

I hope you have had, as we intended, an adventure over old familiar places of play and life during your reading of this book. I hope our words were clear and well-defined. I hope the ideas and concepts will be of some help to you in your efforts to understand and accept your own inner nature as well as that of your complement—your very own perfect fit.

—*Dr. Woods*

Sources/Suggestions for Further Reading

Benjamin, J., Li, L., Patterson, C., Greenberg, B. D., Murphy, D. L., & Hamer, D. H. (1996). Population and familial association between the D4 dopamine receptor gene and measures of novelty seeking. Nature Genetics, 12, 81-84.

Delgado, J. M. R., Roberts, W. W. & Miller, N. E. (1954). Learning motivated by electrical stimulation of the brain. American Journal of Physiology, 179, 587-593.

Ebstein, R. P., Novick, O., Umansky, R., Priel, B., Osher, Y., Blaine, D., Bennett, E. R., Nemanov, L., Katz, M., & Belmaker, R. H. (1996). Dopamine D4 receptor (D4DR) exon III polymorphism associated with the human personality trait of novelty seeking. Nature Genetics, 12, 78-80.

Frank-Kamenetskii, M.D. (1997). *Unraveling DNA: The Most Important Molecule of Life*. Reading, Massachusetts: Addison-Wesley.

Fromm, E. (1965). *Escape From Freedom*. New York: Avon Books, First Printing.

Gallagher, W., (1997). *Just the Way You Are: How Heredity* And *Experience Create The Individual*. New York: Random House, Inc.

Hamer D. & Copeland P. (1998). *Living With Our Genes*. New York: Doubleday.

Kramer P. D. (1993). *Listening To Prozac*. New York: Viking Press.

MacLean, P. D. (1973). A triune concept of the brain and behavior (pp.2-66). In Boag, T. J. & Campbell D., (Eds.), *Hincks Memorial Lectures.* Toronto: University of Toronto Press.

Masson, J. M. & McCarthy, S. (1995). *When Elephants Weep: The Emotional Lives Of Animals.* New York: Delacorte Press.

Masson, J. M. (1997). *Dogs Never Lie About Love.* New York: Crown Publishers, Inc.

Olds, J. & Milner, P. (1954). Positive reinforcement produced by electrical stimulation of septal area and other regions of the rat brain. Journal of Comparative and Physiological Psychology, 47, 419-427.

Roberts, M. (1997). *The Man Who Listens To Horses.* New York: Random House.

Sofer, W. H. (1991). *Introduction To Genetic Engineering.* Newton, Massachusetts: Butterworth-Heinemann.

Stein, L. (1964) Reciprocal action of reward and punishment mechanisms. In R. G. Heath (Ed.) *The Role of Pleasure in Behavior* (pp. 113-139). New York: Harper & Row.

Watson, J. D. (1968). *The Double Helix.* New York: Athenaeum.

Wright, W. (1999). *Born That Way: Genes, Behavior, Personality.* New York: Alfred A. Knopf.

Knapp, C. (1998). *Pack Of Two: The Intricate Bond Between People And Dogs.* New York: Random House.

Table 1: Prominent Tendencies of the Two Basic Temperaments

Be-er	*Do-er*
Lives in the world of the immediate moment; a here-and-now, now-or-never, now-and-always perspective; there is a sense of urgency in the life of the be-er—tasks and goals must be achieved *now or never;* a difficulty putting things on the back burner; may give up easily when persistence over a prolonged period of time is required; paradoxically, may be extremely persistent when fully engaged in a task; compared to the Do-er, the Be-er moves at lightning speed.	Past- and future time-orientation; the present is viewed in light of past pleasures and pains with the expectation of similar outcomes in the future; past mistakes are avoided if possible; past pleasures are sought; a slow, deliberate and patient attitude toward task completion and goal achievement; goals are more easily broken down into interconnected parts of one bigger picture to be achieved slowly over time; confusion when surprised in the here-and-now; compared to the Be-er, the Do-er moves at a snail's pace.

Be-er	Do-er
Surface or liminal processing of psychic feeling resulting in a less weighty experiential past; a difficulty in anticipating future consequences, and greater impulsivity; the experience of psychic pain and psychic pleasure is more in the *doing* and not in the anticipation; a more extroverted, novelty-seeking and daring approach to life.	Deep processing of psychic feeling resulting in a more weighty and meaningful experiential past; may hurt easily but not show it; holds back feeling and reigns in impulses; needs to think things through before acting; a more cautious and introspective approach to life; the experience of psychic pain and psychic pleasure is more anticipatory; the actual occurrence of psychic pain or psychic pleasure serves to reinforce the expectation.
Direct, open, and frank in interpersonal communication; impatient to be heard and a tendency to interrupt; mean what they say and say what they mean in the moment; a tendency to take things at face value; prefers concrete, literal and surface interpretations, e.g. a rose is a rose is a rose.	Communication is indirect and subtle—tends to come to the point slowly approaching tangentially testing the waters; tends to shy away from direct eye contact with others—often looks away, above and below eye level; a tendency to read between the lines for hidden meaning.
Easily distracted by outside stimuli; caught up in happenings in the here and now rather than internal evaluations relating to past and future.	Habituates easily so is not easily distracted by immediate sounds or sights; often unaware of surrounding events due to internal orientation; the present is evaluated in light of past pleasures and pains.
Personally sensitive; trouble separating constructive criticism from personal self; may overreact in the moment; often has difficulty appreciating statements said in humor as takes them seriously—hurts easily; often described as perceptive versus empathic.	More able to be empathic; easily tunes in to the feelings emanating from others; may feel very close and empathic with others, however, on a surface, physical level, tends to be hesitant and awkward; may hurt easily but tends not to show it.

Be-er	Do-er
Spontaneous; seeks physical closeness and open, direct expressions of feeling; seeks the limelight where they are more likely to get the feeling attention they need; personal space (buffer zone) requirements are considerably less compared to the Do-er.	Less spontaneous; less demonstrative; more laid back; uncomfortable with public displays of affection preferring privacy for such matters; requires much personal space (buffer zone) relative to the Be-er; needs to withdraw from the banquet of social experience from time to time in order to think things through and shed any overload of feeling.
More reliant on the attitudes and opinions of others in evaluating objects, events and goals.	Tendency to keep their own council; less reliant on the opinions and attitudes of others.
View of others on a horizontal axis, e.g., relates to the janitor and the CEO of a company in same egalitarian manner.	Evaluation of others on a vertical axis needing to see where they stand, i.e., superior or inferior.
Difficulty competing—needs to win at all costs; uncomfortable sharing the limelight.	Competes easily, however, competition is more about beating the opponent rather than winning.
Seeks feeling attention from others no matter what the tone; considering the cooler inner life of the Be-er, bad feeling is better than no feeling so may push others with negative behavior if good feeling is not forthcoming.	Situations that stimulate bad feeling are avoided if at all possible; if escape is not possible, may react with anger and even physical aggression.

About the Author

Sandra K. Woods has a PhD in psychology with a concentration in neuroscience from the University of Massachusetts at Amherst. She has over thirty years of experience in the field during which time she worked as a director of a sheltered workshop for the developmentally disabled, a school psychologist, a consulting psychologist, a psychiatrist assistant, a psychotherapist working extensively with couples and families, and an adjunct lecturer at the University of Massachusetts at Amherst. She met Willis H. Ploof, MD in the late 60s following her early graduate training (Springfield College, Springfield, Massachusetts) in rehabilitation counseling and clinical psychology. She and Dr. Ploof collaborated on various projects until his death in 1996. Together they wrote ***Understanding ADHD: Attention Deficit Hyperactivity Disorder and the Feeling Brain*** which was published in 1997 (Sage Publications, Thousand Oaks, CA). In 2007 she retired and now lives in Western Massachusetts with her dog, Molly.

About Willis H. Ploof, MD

Willis H. Ploof retired from private practice in the early 90s to concentrate on his writing. During his long professional career, he was responsible for the establishment of two community-based mental health clinics, one in Holyoke, Massachusetts, and the other in Kingsport, Tennessee. During the Korean War, he served as chief psychiatrist at the Army Disciplinary Barracks in Harrisburg, Pennsylvania. For many years, he served as consultant to the Massachusetts Rehabilitation Commission and to the Youthful Offender Program at Goodwill Industries, Springfield, Massachusetts. In the late 60s Dr. Ploof established and supervised the Pupil Adjustment Program for the Springfield School Department, a comprehensive program designed to treat children with symptoms of Attention Deficit Hyperactivity Disorder. During his career, he also worked extensively with married couples and families. He received his MD from Boston University School of Medicine and did his training in the practice of child, adolescent, and adult psychiatry under Elvin Semrad, Felix Deutch, and Joseph Weinreb.